For All You Do

For All You Do

Self-Care and Encouragement for Teachers

Peter Mishler

Andrews McMeel
PUBLISHING®

To my Mother
thirty-two-year veteran

To my Father
twenty-five years of advocacy

Introduction

The modern teacher is faced with a monumental responsibility. Setting aside the challenges of meeting our students' educational needs, we often find ourselves playing additional roles as surrogate counselors, social workers, student advocates, and substitute caretakers, while also facing down our society's burdens, including gun violence, the effects of childhood trauma, and painful social inequities.

To do this work well takes a remarkable person— someone who is not only willing to learn how to teach all of their students well, but one who is also dedicated to compassion, empathy, and a sense of justice these additional roles require.

Unsurprisingly then, we teachers have to handle a lot of stress. We are fortunate that the work we love engages our hearts, minds, and spirits; yet, for that very reason, it can be exceptionally draining and often forces us to make personal sacrifices for the well-being of our students.

And that's during normal, non-pandemic times.

If nothing else, the 2020-2021 school year has demonstrated to us teachers—likely more than ever— that we will always be called upon to shoulder whatever challenges our world presents.

Perhaps this is why we keep hearing the line, *Thanks for all you do*. If you've taught for a day, you know this phrase well. You've likely seen it in a card or an email. It fits perfectly on a cake for the faculty room. It's the polite, courteous, obligatory thing to say when someone wants to thank a teacher for anything. Basically, it's our version of *Thank you for your service.*

A catchphrase like this, especially the more it's repeated, begins to sound meaningless, but I think it at least points to the fact that although most people don't exactly know everything we do, they do realize we're doing it. And that's really important. I'll take it. I'll take all the thanks I can get!

But in this challenging and intense profession, we know that thank-yous are sometimes not enough. Even though the thought matters, we teachers are often left with a ton of *Thanks for all you dos* (and gift cards and candy and coffee mugs) and our own tanks still on empty.

Working for the well-being of others can leave us wanting. Therefore, I think it's time we examine "all we do" a little differently—not for acknowledgment or recognition or thanks—but to discover the ways the many roles we play can reveal opportunities to benefit and give back to ourselves.

But don't worry. I know what you're thinking. Before you cringe at *self-care* in the subtitle, I want you to know that the entries in this book do not ask you to take on any more than you're already doing. There seems to be a trend in our culture that in order to feel balanced, happy, and well, we need to jump on self-care the way we dive into our teaching.

The new "self-care culture" can overwhelm. We teachers are already swamped with extras. It's not time to add to our to-do lists or overburden ourselves. It is time for us to look at all we do now and use these experiences to slightly shift our perspective, remembering that the work we're doing not only benefits others but ourselves as well.

And that's exactly what this book seeks to offer. In the pages that follow, I've collected the many stories, experiences, and observations from my teaching life that demonstrate all we do, from the beginning of my day to the end, from the first day of school to the last, from the highs to the lows.

Each piece is followed by a reflection that offers something we can keep for ourselves, whether it's emphasizing how significant and powerful our roles as teachers really are, revealing the timeless truths hidden within our day-to-day work, suggesting ways to protect ourselves from common stressors, or providing affirmations and other tools for personal growth.

To make this easy for our harried teaching lives, this is a book you can flip through to find what you need *when you need it*.

There's no pressure here, no program. This is *our time* to reflect, meditate, and care for ourselves as we're able. In writing this book, I was struck by the benefits of reflecting on myself as a person and a teacher. I hope that you will find something here that will be helpful to you too.

From one teacher to another, I see you for all you do. May we continue to take care of ourselves in the ways that work for us so we can carry on in this profession we love.

On What Matters

In my day-to-day work, I am often overwhelmed by the many parts of my teaching life that are *not* teaching— the paperwork, committees, meetings, and initiatives. On top of this, there are the particular interpersonal dramas of the year that can get the best of me, even when I tell myself at the end of each summer that this will be the year I'll just go in, do my job well, ignore the noise, and head out the door. And that's not to mention the preparation of lessons, planning, and grading that get me thinking surgically: "If we do *this* by next Monday, then I'll have time for *this*, but then I'll have to cut *that*..." With all of this in my head, I start to miss the point of it all—and fast. I think my record right now is about two weeks of teaching bliss at the beginning of the school year before the stress creeps in.

It's been important to remind myself of what I really deep down love about my work. This may seem a little simplistic and self-helpy, but for me, when I do it, I feel refocused and refreshed. It reminds me of what really matters, especially when I stray so far away from what I value about teaching as the year progresses.

I love teaching because it is a creative act, a kind of puzzle that preoccupies my imagination: how do I find the best, most interesting way to help my students learn something new? And to then see students succeed at doing something they didn't think they were capable of before—that's the payoff.

Each of us has our own answer to what matters to us as teachers. Answering this question from time to time can begin the process of turning the volume down on what doesn't matter, even if those pitfalls—the bureaucracy, the drama, the grind—are unavoidable. Writing down what I value even now reengages me.

In reminding myself of what matters, I am giving myself a chance to regroup so that the days ahead can be a demonstration of what I know makes a difference in the lives of my students and leaves me feeling fulfilled in my career.

Reflection: *There are times when I need to take stock of what matters most—what I value most—knowing that this gives me a chance to re-center my teaching. Today I will look for practical ways to let what I love back into my teaching and find ways to diminish those aspects of my professional life that do not serve me or my students well.*

On the Teacher's Workday

I've heard it said that teachers can have a forty-hour workweek, too, if they learn some balance. Often, however, teaching is just not the kind of job we can leave on our desk until morning.

Even when we don't physically bring our school day home with us, it occupies our minds, hearts, and spirits, and that's because I think there's something very important to recognize about our work as teachers.

We are not just professionals—we are practicing an art form.

The planning of a lesson itself is much like making a piece of art—it comes together over multiple attempts and expressions and requires distance, time, imagination, and persistence. And like most creative endeavors, it doesn't operate on a specific schedule.

Teaching is also an act of strategy, insight, and the balancing of ever-changing dynamics. It is essential to our profession that we constantly prepare for scenarios that may or may not come to pass. In fact, even when we're in the middle of teaching, we are still thinking and creating while navigating several relationships with students as well as their relationships with each other, while also trying to think of ways we can modify a lesson on the fly that we've already taken much time to plan.

Teachers, therefore, are always clocked in, whether we're planning or preparing and whether or not we're in the classroom. Although it'd be nice to leave my work in a drawer more often, I certainly wouldn't want to lose what makes teaching more of a calling than a job, more of an art form than a profession.

When I want to relax and can't seem to shake thinking about school, I can at least tell myself that it's not simply because I'm off balance. I can gently remind myself instead that teaching's still on my mind because teaching is a creative and compassionate act. It wakes one up in the middle of the night, just the same as every true exercise of the mind, heart, and spirit.

Reflection: *The practice of noticing and accepting that my teacher-mind is constantly working to meet the demands of the job is helpful for me to try. It helps me see that my mind is not running because I'm flawed. It might just be that I'm constantly thinking because I'm a creative teacher. By recognizing this truth, I can be gentler with myself and feel pride in having a job that requires my intellectual and imaginative resources.*

On Saying Yes

Today, I am thinking about a student named "S." She very much wanted to be involved in a challenging project I had reserved for students who had already completed certain aspects of the curriculum I was required to teach.

S. made her interest in this project known to me on a few occasions, going out of her way to tell me how exciting she thought it would be and asking if she could try it.

I have to be honest about my first response—I told her I wasn't sure it was a good idea.

I had some fair points: I wanted to ensure she had some skills under her belt that I didn't want her to leave my class without. I thought it would be a disservice to her to move on to something I didn't think she was quite ready for.

And yet, she kept asking. She let me know she had already considered several ideas she'd like to explore. Unlike other students who *were* "ready" for this experience, S. was engaging me in ways they were not.

I reflected on my initial reaction to S. Why would I prevent a student from doing something they find so appealing? It's not every day I have a student both willing and thrilled about their learning and who is confidently advocating for themselves.

No, I thought again. *This is the way students lose out on essential skills they need. I can't engage her interests at the expense of what I know she will need later.*

And yet, all of this sounded ridiculous to me as I spelled it out in my head. It looks ridiculous on paper now. I realized then, although it seems so obvious now, that I was missing an opportunity with S.

So I let her begin the project. She beamed. And that was enough for me. We worked together as I found ways to integrate the skills I wanted to ensure she learned while she embarked eagerly on this new creative work. In fact, she likely wouldn't have learned those skills I wanted her to have without access to this special project.

But did S. leave my class with everything she needed as a learner? Good question. Probably not. However, I know for sure she hasn't imploded without my "skills."

I have to imagine that S., after winning my confidence, praise, and a chance to do something she loved—in short, advocating for herself and having an adult tell her, "Yes"— was as essential an experience as any curricular skill I could have dreamed up. I believe this "yes" was far more beneficial than the supposed wisdom of my "no."

Reflection: *While I often think I know what is best for my students, I have to remember to keep the door open for the unexpected, especially if there is an opportunity to make a difference in a student's life in a way I hadn't intended or that goes against some philosophy of teaching or "better judgment." May I always have the openness and flexibility to provide for my students in ways I can't yet imagine.*

On Refreshing the Art of Teaching

The beginning of the year is a time of excitement for teachers: new students, new ideas, new ways to make the old material fresh again.

However, as my work with students progresses, even a few weeks later, I find myself out of time, resources, and energy to maintain that vigor.

This is fine. It's completely okay. It's hard for anyone to hit the restart button midstride.

But as someone who feels engaged with his teaching when experimenting with new ideas, I try to find ways to make things fresh again. I start small, reading new books or articles in my area of expertise, even a little at a time.

These actions help me gain new insights or enthusiasm that I want to bring back to the classroom. And I always feel excited again when I'm learning new things about the subject I thought I knew so well.

Finding a simple way to get back to those feelings can be a sustaining force for us as the real, hard, day-to-day work of teaching sets in.

Reflection: *I often tell my students that incremental changes can bring about good results. Today I will follow this advice myself by taking a practical step toward feeling newly engaged in my teaching.*

On Simplicity

Today, while buckling my daughter into her car seat, she told me that the lead teacher from her preschool is a "really, really great teacher."

I asked her why.

"Because she knows everything," my daughter said.

But I wasn't satisfied. "You're right," I said. "But what does she *do* that makes your teacher so special to you?"

"Well," my daughter straightened, "she helps me with everything and checks on me and has a beautiful voice and is always smiling at me."

I thought, *It really is that simple, isn't it, how to be a great teacher, how to educate a child? I make it so complicated.*

Truly, there is nothing more I could ever ask of my daughter's teacher than what she described in the car.

Imagine a classroom where each student knows we are checking on them, always there to help, and doing so with kindness and warmth (the beautiful voice thing is maybe just a bonus). I'd unequivocally say that this is a classroom where students would want to be and one where learning is happening—a place where students would feel safe to be themselves and to grow.

I noticed a common theme among my teacher friends when we returned to the classroom after an anguishing summer of 2020 trying to figure out whether schools would be open, what our district's policies would be, whether we'd feel safe, how to operate the technology for remote learning, and what it would all be like.

But once my teacher friends and I got back to the classroom, I did notice some relief in our voices. The anxiety and buildup and logistical stress were lessened by the experience of being with our students.

Of course, it hasn't been, and never will be, all that easy day to day. But the power in those basic tenets my daughter articulated so simply can be a game-changer for us too.

A good, simple job description for teachers: check on students, help them, and do it with warmth and care.

Reflection: *Human beings like to be helped and sense they are being cared for. This is true for the youngest child as well as the adult who is returning to school after years away. In this simplicity is where teachers often find a reward; participating in an act that is helpful to others can simultaneously help dissolve our difficulties too.*

On the Power of Authenticity

One of my favorite classroom moments occurred in my first year in education. I was teaching a very challenging group of teenagers who were shockingly uninvested in my novice attempt at teaching Old English poetry.

Mid-lesson, however, I thought of what was likely my first good question as a teacher. But it was one I hadn't thought of in advance or written down! Up to that point, everything I said or did in class was straight from the script.

I told my students I was about to ask them a question I didn't know how to ask. Then I told them I didn't know the answer. At first, they laughed.

Then I went for it, thinking out loud. The room truly went silent. There was a palpable energy present. I felt in that moment like a "real teacher."

Then I started to answer my question a little at a time. I told them I found the question very difficult. And it was then that they took this on as a challenge.

A few started offering answers. Then more. Others even thought of ways to rephrase the question to make it clearer. I was getting exactly what I wanted from my students. Class ended with students writing down answers for me, anxious to see if they were "right."

To this day, I think about why this worked. I think it's because I had provided, for the first time, a real question to which I genuinely wanted to know the answer, and, further, I was willing to put my twenty-seven-year-old, khaki-and-tie self on the line to demonstrate how thinking and learning worked for me. In short, I gave them something real.

Now obviously, this was a perfect-storm scenario. The idea of *Be curious!* and *Learn right beside them!* is cute, but it works better in a tweet than in the actual day-to-day classroom. But I was inspired after that day to continue searching for ways to provide natural learning scenarios for my students. Even if I can't conjure these experiences daily (I can't), I now know they are attainable, real, and worthwhile.

Reflection: *I am at my best and feel most free when I am being myself in the classroom. The times I've felt this freedom have been some of the most effective and rewarding moments of my teaching life. Today I will consider ways to bring my most natural, authentic self to the classroom and my lessons, knowing it is a service to my students when I show them that learning is a real part of who I am and not merely a performance.*

On "My" Students

I love taking credit for my students when they're succeeding. And, if I'm being honest, I know how to distance myself from them with excuses when they're not.

In either case, these reactions tell me that I'm operating under the false premise that my students are a reflection of me, which is a nice way of saying I think I'm more powerful than I am.

It is important to reflect on the complex experiences, people, and events that contribute to how a student learns and finds success, many of which lie outside of my lessons and guidance.

Yes, we play our part. A leading part. But as an exercise, I try to single out one important skill I've learned as a student, and I try to remember when I learned it. Then, I try to identify all the other factors involved in my learning, including those that occurred outside the classroom or long before that moment in time. This helps me to consider that a student's success is likely a collaboration of many influences and not necessarily the work of just one individual teacher.

I will always have a very meaningful part to play in the lives of my students, but how much more openhearted and satisfied I feel as a teacher when I can see that my students know they are not just expected to perform for me—when they know I see them as people, and not "my students," and when I remember that their road to success is built with many bricks, not just mine.

Reflection: *While I am responsible for the students I teach, it is also relieving to know—contrary to what I sometimes believe—that I do not have to be in control of everything they are learning in my classroom. Today I will see my students' learning for its complexity. I will strive for the wisdom to know my role in their learning and to relinquish the roles that are not mine to take on.*

On Giving Students Some Room

The first time I had to speak in front of a group of teachers, I discovered it's really a lot like speaking to a group of students. They don't always pay attention, they check their phones a lot, and they have the kinds of side conversations that might elicit the classic cliché teacher quip, "I'll wait until you're finished."

It occurred to me then that if this is how adults generally behave (and I think there is good evidence to show this is not exclusive to teachers), maybe I should reconsider my expectations for students. My impulse, early in my teaching career, was to shut down the first spark of an off-topic conversation or a lack of focus from students, mostly out of fear that students weren't respecting me or that someone would happen to walk by and assume students weren't engaged.

However, if I can fully erase the conception that students are things to be molded, then I also have to accept what is natural human behavior. The stuff we might reprimand students for in the classroom is often considered normal behavior out in the world. Young students need that same leeway we would afford adults. They also deserve leeway for what we know is true of students of any given age: students are always going to do student-like things.

Of course, there is something to be said for being considerate, and I do think part of our responsibility as teachers is to cultivate these values responsibly and thoughtfully in those we teach, but my observations about how the very adults who are meant to be examples of maturity behave have given me some room to give my students some room.

I feel a sense of relief and pride that I've been able to gain more and more awareness of how to treat my students well, especially considering that I grew up under, and was certainly molded by, the belief that teachers are disciplinarians as much as they are knowledgeable about their content. And besides, giving my students room—to be understanding of the inclinations that make them humans, not "pupils"—is more likely to garner the respect I am looking for, which is mutual.

Reflection: *Seeing my students from new perspectives— whatever they may be—is often a matter of empathy and respect. I am fortunate that I can continually evolve in my understanding of people and how I interact with them because of my role as a teacher. I can become a more understanding, open person as a result of my teaching.*

On Having the Perfect Words

There are times when a student needs to connect about a problem or struggle they're having. These are the moments when I notice my brain trying desperately to conjure the absolute perfect words that will set this student back on their feet.

This thinking is the result of having seen too many inspirational teacher movies. You know the ones: the unorthodox teacher comes to town, forms a bond with a troubled kid, and gives them an impassioned speech that changes the child for good.

I've very rarely had one of these conversations. Usually, by the end of our talk, I have the sneaking suspicion that I didn't nail it. And that's right; I probably didn't. No single conversation with a student will evolve into award-winning dialogue. It's more likely that a series of events and experiences and loving people will collaborate in helping this student with their needs. It's more likely that my consistent, naturally unfolding relationship with this student will be more powerful than any single speech.

Most of the time, I can feel good about my usefulness in these conversations if I focus on what I can control: my presence, my willingness, my honesty, and my care.

Then, out of the blue, I hear from a former student—one I wouldn't expect—and, without having planned it, it turns out I did give them that Hollywood speech they needed.

Reflection: *I do not need to have the perfect speech, advice, or guidance for my students. I only need the strength to show up for them as a continuous, caring presence in their lives. Today, in each opportunity that reveals itself, I will aim to be as helpful and present for my students as I can.*

On the Stigmas of Teaching

I admit I sometimes have a sense of unease when I tell others I'm a teacher. I am already anticipating what they'll say about my "summers off," or comment on how little I'm paid, or rope me in with their worst schooling experiences. And let's not forget the old "those who can't do" line. I'll never understand what compels someone to offer up that little gem.

Often, I'll smile and nod sheepishly when I hear some variation on the above. But as I've grown into my role as a teacher more confidently, my understanding of the work I do has revealed itself, and sometimes I need to remind myself of these positive truths, especially in the face of comments like these. I need to replace my feelings of discomfort about how others see teaching.

I know very well this profession's rich rewards, joys, and irreplaceable value. I know them by heart, and I have the stories to prove it. I know what it looks like to capture my students' imaginations, to see them thrive despite dire situations, and what it's like to receive my students' actual gratitude and trust. I know what it means to fulfill a necessary role in a young person's life.

It is my responsibility to make *these* experiences known to those I meet instead of being complicit in reinforcing teacher stereotypes by not speaking up, by smiling and nodding. I'm hardworking, trustworthy, and what I "do" in nine months is what many "do" in two years. Knowing how deeply I've contributed to the actual lives of my students, I should respond to misrepresentations about my profession with the confidence of the heart surgeon, not the humble schoolteacher.

Reflection: *I deserve to own the narrative about the reality of my teaching life. Today I will look for opportunities to speak with pride about what I know to be true. I will begin to construct a more confident and affirming story of myself and my life as a teacher.*

On a Receptive Approach to Students

When my wife was pregnant with our first child, I would often muse about what I thought our baby would be like, and I imagined a kind of narrative about her personality, however harmlessly.

"Let's just wait to meet her," my wife said. "And she'll let us know who she is."

I found my wife's comment striking as it relates to parenting, and I also find it useful as a teacher seeking to understand, advocate for, and meet the needs of my students.

I have to admit I sometimes fall into the trap of seeing my students as a single group and, in error, encouraging them toward a standardized endpoint.

There are times when I find myself overly influenced by the ever-encroaching standardized tests, curriculum standards, and mandates whose educational demands and endgames take their unconscious toll on me. It's only natural; these are the stressors that drive education in general.

It may seem obvious, but even when I am working to understand how to reach a learner in my classroom, I still might have the tendency—while caught in the fast-paced machinations of the school year—to think, *So, how can I help them fit the mold?* And yet, this approach makes an assumption about the kind of success that is right for any particular student and tells me I may be overlooking or failing to reimagine what access to a fulfilling learning experience looks like for that student.

Our students have much to tell us, and we have much to understand, whether it is about their disabilities, accommodations and considerations for accessibility, interests and goals, personal definitions of success, educational and life experiences, the way they see the world—and all of this knowledge allow us to envision the best way forward for each student.

My wife's wise approach, which is *receptive* and not assertive, suggests that meeting and receiving our students as they are does not have a particular outcome in mind. Instead of spending creative energy on finding ways to fit each student into the more narrow and time-efficient definitions of success that often await them, I can find release from my own urgent expectations (and that of the larger educational system) with each small contribution to educational advocacy I make on behalf of my students— and this begins with allowing each of them the time, space, and respect to speak first.

Reflection: *My career is more fulfilling than I ever could have imagined, especially when I am challenging my own perceptions of what's best for my students. I find that when I am open to new approaches, I am not only a more effective advocate for my students, but I feel a sense of excitement about the freedom and possibility that is available to me in this profession.*

On How Students Learn

As someone who is constantly working on the art of writing, I can personally attest to the fact that learning does not occur in a straight line. I've never graduated from Skill 1.1, then moved directly to Skill 1.2, and then, having accomplished 1.2, moved on to 1.3 in a linear progression.

While there is, of course, the obvious value in learning skills sequentially, my experience tells me there is great importance in learning that happens under far less organized circumstances.

I think of all the things about writing I chose not to learn or was unable to, which later became necessary and even desirable for me to learn when I started writing professionally.

Not boxed into a specific timeframe or test, I was able to relearn with space and freedom and breathing room needed to experiment and fail and try again. Better yet, I had the willingness to learn those skills for a specific, meaningful purpose. I've had the same experience when learning how to teach. I became a far better student of reading when I knew I had to teach those skills to my classes.

It is helpful for me to recognize the organic, nonsequential, and individual nature of learning.

When I recognize this truth, I am more patient with my students, and I feel freer to give them more freedom and room. It also makes me very happy to know that the book is never fully written on what my students are capable of.

Reflection: *I can give myself a break about the anxieties of teaching "just right." Today I will look more closely at the diverse and individual ways of learning that are present in my classroom and identify ways to champion this diversity in my planning, teaching, and interactions with students.*

On Vulnerability

Uncertainty and vulnerability about how my teaching is going or what my students think of me are two of my least favorite feelings, even though I should know by now that they're just facts of our profession.

I admit I've found ways to cope with feeling insecure in the classroom that I'm not proud of. More than once, I've pretended I was asking students to reflect on their learning, but what I really wanted to know was if they thought I was any good. I've even "happened to walk by" another teacher's classroom to see if they were doing things better than I could.

What I'm missing when I feel and act this way is a recognition of how normal and natural these feelings of uncertainty and vulnerability are. Of course, they're normal! We're at center stage every day, performing for sometimes up to hundreds of learners of all kinds and asking them to take risks, grow, and improve at something they may or may not be all that excited about.

To recognize how normal these feelings of uncertainty are—and to understand the reality of how vulnerable teaching makes us—is empowering for me. It begins to de-escalate the imagined crisis of professional inadequacy that I believe is mine alone.

I can also recognize that these feelings pass. The next thing I know, I'll get a note or an email or a compliment, and everything's changed.

Reflection: *It is normal to feel self-conscious and uncomfortable as a teacher. The very nature of the profession lends itself to these feelings. Today I will notice how the challenges of my position would make anyone, even the "experts," uncertain or uncomfortable. I will remember that I have also felt the highs and experienced the rewards that result from those very same challenges.*

On Providing Safety for Safety's Sake

We often talk about how all students have the right to learn, and, for this learning to occur, that our students must first feel safe, sheltered, and protected.

Sometimes we have to put academic learning to the side for a time. Sometimes our love and care for our students' safety *is* the lesson we're teaching.

To walk through the world knowing some people have actively shown us their love when we needed it the most can be far more valuable than any academic lesson we can learn. The academic lesson can likely come elsewhere, at another time—but love is sometimes scarce.

Until there are more and richer resources available to shore up the needs of the vulnerable, the responsibility of safety and protection often arrives at our classroom door. So many of our students need us and our classrooms to be places of shelter, and learning may not always be on the table right away.

I think particularly of my LGBTQIA+ students who have come out, only to face the rejection of those who were supposed to love them unconditionally. I think of the students who have used my classroom as a place to rest their minds and bodies in the aftermath of violence at home or in our community. In these circumstances and so many others, my curriculum, for a time, did not matter. In each case, I thought, *If my classroom can serve as a safeguard for these students—if only for a bell period each day—I know I will have done my job well.*

I can't romanticize "safety" as a means to the desired end result of learning. If this is my tactic, then I am touting love and care with another motive in mind when my students need someone they can trust. I believe that if caring for my students really matters to me, I need to trust in this as an end in itself, no matter the outcome . . . and no matter the optics. It may, in fact, appear as if the student isn't "engaged," an anxiety we face when we are visited by administrators and observers who want to see us perform. In these cases, I have had to work on standing firm in my decision to provide a safe space first.

At times, yes, my vulnerable students have done me one better by showing interest in class once their more immediate needs were met, and it is certainly affirming to know I have encouraged them and can now provide for them doubly. But what about my vulnerable students who aren't eventually able to learn effectively in my classroom? They still have my unwavering protection. And what an affirming thing it is to know that this kind of unconditional protection is in my power to provide.

Reflection: *It is profoundly humbling to know I have the responsibility to provide forms of shelter and safety for my students. This opportunity does not fall on the shoulders of just anyone. Today I will consider the ways that I can protect the students in my care, even if these students' circumstances require nontraditional support.*

On the Need for Breaks

Teachers are rewarded with ample breaks during the school year, and these, of course, are the subject of tiresome complaints from non-educators.

Our breaks are often used as the public's justification for our profession's low wages, as well as the reason why they sometimes call our jobs a cakewalk or a pretty sweet deal.

I see these breaks a little differently. Our time away from the classroom restores us from a difficulty that is particular to our profession: receiving and bearing the stress of others.

Teachers are tasked daily with taking on all our students' needs, large or small, routine or acute. We do this work well, and yet, it's difficult work, and I think it takes more of a toll than I've given it credit for because I don't think of it as *my* stress—it's someone else's pain I'm helping to heal.

As far as I know, however, it doesn't work this way. Teachers, empathetic by nature, are affected deeply too. It is hard to see people worried, anxious, struggling, or suffering, and it is hard to know that our power to help has its limits.

We need significant breaks, then, to give ourselves a chance to be restored, to be unburdened, to become lighter in our bodies, and to live our lives, knowing that when we return, we will be charged with the same noble and necessary challenges once again.

Reflection: *In a career that requires significant dedication to the needs of others, we, too, need to be rested and restored to do our work well. May I take time to unwind and care for myself so I can return refreshed to my students.*

On Being New

One of the most difficult parts of being a new teacher is when we recognize there are many layers to our profession that require our attention and energy. Teaching—what we fell in love with about the job in the first place—is only a beginning.

We have to get acclimated to the rhythms by which a school building runs: the routines, systems, structures, and dynamics. Then, there are our relationships with the many staff members we will work with, in and out of the building. As with most careers, getting used to these aspects alone requires a significant amount of mental energy. Being new anywhere is hard.

From there, we enter our classrooms, our havens, and soon discover that our work in this space is made up of two individual jobs. There's the planning, preparation, and reflection that come before we arrive and after we leave; then, there's the teaching itself.

We also engage in more occasional work, whether it is with parents or in extracurriculars we decide to take on or feel obligated to try so we can make ourselves valuable to the school community—not to mention our role in ensuring that building initiatives and programs are fulfilled.

It's a lot. *It's a lot.*

Say what you want about the fumbling, anxious, insecure new teacher. I have the highest respect for anyone who wants to take on this job and learn how to do it well because I think this says something very special about us.

Those who teach have the strength to take on the multiple layers of work required to do this job successfully.

Those who teach are people who show up anyway, even when our early days in the profession can be nerve-wracking and even terrifying.

Those who teach persist in the face of the times we are questioned or dismissed by students or parents because we are new; despite this, we still want to help our students find success.

Those who teach are willing to learn an art form that can take years to develop and hone.

Those who teach are willing to learn an art form. That alone is rare.

These qualities are what I've seen from nearly every new teacher I've met, and, for this reason alone, I am proud to be an educator. When someone chooses to become a teacher, we should be celebrating the fact that our culture can produce the kind of person who, through their courage, resilience, and commitment, will directly impact the health and well-being of others.

Reflection: *Whether I am a brand-new teacher, a teacher who is making a transition to a new learning environment, or a veteran who has the opportunity to encourage or mentor those coming into the profession, may I remember how remarkable and strong I am for taking on a role that is centered not in self, but in care and support for others.*

On Time Spent Elsewhere

One of the best years of my teaching career followed the summer I spent traveling in the United States and Canada. I wrote, walked cities, visited museums, met new people, spent time with distant family and friends, camped, hiked, and swam.

I returned to school rested and eager to teach again. A journal I kept on my trip proved useful, and I was able to adapt that writing into new concepts for my courses. I had new materials, books, and ideas. Having thoroughly departed physically and emotionally from my classroom for a few months, I felt like I'd been gone for a year.

During the school year, I often find myself enmeshed in my school's culture and routines in ways that can strip my identity down to Guy Who Plans, Teaches, Grades, and Plans Some More. I persuade myself that my many hours logged at school make me a better teacher, but, ultimately, there are ways in which I'm mistaken. Spending so much time in a school building does not make me my best, healthiest self. I lose a large part of me in that world, even as I am likely being helpful to others.

I don't often get new ideas for teaching, and I can't restore myself when I'm steeped in school. My best teaching comes from adult conversation, experiencing my community, doing new things, and literally "getting away." And it doesn't need to be a grand plan or trip. There are many manageable and practical ways to dip out of the teaching game. The litmus test for me is if I'm able to cancel out my brain's typical feed of school thoughts. When I can replace that thinking, I know I've been successful.

The more time I spend outside of school, the more enriched I feel, and the more natural, authentic, and inspired I am as a teacher. My students benefit most from having a living, breathing, engaged adult in their lives, and not the "me" who is only a bleary-eyed teacher.

Reflection: *My refreshed, alert, engaged self is the one I prefer to bring to my teaching. Though it is difficult to achieve this as we immerse ourselves in the daily challenges of our work, making time to feel whole again, especially socially and intellectually, makes teaching a place where we offer a piece of our best self as opposed to a place where that best self fades.*

On Meditation and the Day Ahead

Basic meditation is a practice that has benefited me as an educator. And I try to keep it very simple.

In the mornings before teaching, I spend about five minutes focusing on my body, breathing, and thinking.

The goal for me is to bring these parts of myself into the present moment in a calming, quiet, comfortable space.

But it isn't always easy.

My mornings are usually all about "what's next." My body is already itching to get out the door, my breathing is already quickening to meet the expectations of the morning, and I'm thinking a dozen things in anticipation of the day ahead.

Therefore, I find I have to get myself to "return" to the present moment in body, breath, and mind, and I have to make this return continually during this meditation time.

To return to the present, I focus on the in and out of my breath, even as my body and especially my mind want to be anywhere else.

And that's my basic practice. That's it.

And it *is* practice.

What's the benefit to me as a teacher? I've noticed that when I try this consistently, something happens in me.

When I find myself in a situation at school that demands my attention and focus, whether it's being able to react attentively to my students, listening well, or managing some problem that's likely to arise, I notice that this brief, imperfect morning practice of returning to the present moment allows me to be more alert and aware in the parts of the day when my presence is most necessary.

By practicing meditation, I can provide for my students' needs with more attention and with less intensity or stress, which in turn brings more fulfillment, satisfaction, and purpose to this teacher who wants to give his very best to his students each day.

Reflection: *There are many ways to increase my energy, care, and focus on the work in front of me, and many of these are time-honored practices that have been used for centuries. Whatever the practice might be, may I have the willingness to seek out what works for me to feel sustained, attentive, and able to meet the day of teaching ahead.*

On Falling Short

I am writing this having just ended a morning remote-learning session with my students. It was kind of a disaster. First off, I started the class after only one cup of coffee instead of my normal two because I was running behind (toddlers).

Then, a new student joined us, and having previously contacted him to ensure I was pronouncing his name correctly, I pronounced it the way he told me it was *definitely not* pronounced in an earlier email.

Flustered by my mistake, I moved on to the lesson and found myself bumbling through an explanation of comma usage (I know), and as I tried to provide examples for students from my head—something I'd planned to do—the sentences I wrote for them grew increasingly complex and convoluted, which ultimately led to my being corrected by a student because my work was just flat-out wrong. Embarrassed, but choosing to keep the hits coming, I decided, instead of accepting the correction, to explain that *hypothetically* there was perhaps some "gray area" between my answer and theirs (there isn't).

The lesson ended with me rolling out an assignment, which required more clarification than I was expecting, and, after weathering some questions as well as an additional correction or two from students, I ended our session addled, uncaffeinated, hungry, dejected, and beginning to type an apology to the student I'd introduced incorrectly.

Is it likely my students left the meeting thinking I was a fool? The worst teacher they'd ever had? A failure? A sham? The "real me" finally exposed? I doubt it. But that's how I felt.

My first instinct was, *How am I going to fix this feeling*? But then I reminded myself that students see my classes with less scrutiny and over-seriousness than I do, for there's more to their lives than the hour they're spending with me. This calmed me down a little. I also reminded myself that I've been here before. This feeling of falling short is less frequent than it used to be, but I know that fumbling desperately through a lesson is just a normal part of teaching—and it's also a discomfort that will eventually go away.

The best news? I am meeting a new group of students this afternoon, and we'll be doing the same lesson. The day after tomorrow, I return to the group from this morning. I'm looking forward to amending some of my silliness then and, without overcompensating, getting things just a little more "right," starting with that second coffee.

Reflection: *Making mistakes and falling short are completely normal experiences for a teacher, and so are the feelings of embarrassment or unworthiness that can come with them. May I have the strength to accept these situations and the feelings that accompany them when they arise, and may I use the kind of bravery we teachers have in spades to step up and try it all again.*

On Sharing the Burden

Not too many days go by before I encounter a colleague who is experiencing some difficult emotion, whether it's frustration, anger, sadness, fear, resentment, hurt feelings, or some other completely normal feeling we teachers can have in the intensity of our day-to-day work.

And so I look for opportunities to share my experiences with another teacher who is struggling. We all know there's nothing quite like talking with someone who understands, who can match their experience to ours, and who can take away some of the stings of whatever we're experiencing.

Sharing with another teacher helps me feel that my worst moments as a teacher can still be useful. Though I may not be able to fix the problem, sharing is also a way of normalizing stressful feelings that all teachers have. That in itself can be healing.

This isn't some new idea, I know. But it is an important one to remember on the front lines of teaching—a place where quite literally anything can happen. I am always heartened to find solidarity and strength when I rely on and help carry my colleagues in this unique profession. This sharing sustains us, and when we feel sustained, we can return refreshed to what we find joyful about the work we do.

Reflection: *I am always uplifted when I am being candid with another teacher, either to help them or talk out my own difficulties. Today I will remember the value of these connections and be aware of opportunities to forge such relationships when they present themselves.*

On Resilience

At the start of my fourth year of teaching, I was sure I wasn't going to last. I've suffered from a panic disorder since I was a teenager, but that September, it owned me intensely. My biggest fear was that I would panic in class and not know what I was going to say in front of my students. Then—all of them looking at me—I'd be trapped in the room with nowhere to run. Compounding this, I was certain I'd then be called on the carpet for my failure, and my success up to that point would be written off; they'd know the *real* me, the one who was actually "crazy" and couldn't teach. I'd be exposed.

I couldn't eat. I had difficulty sleeping. I was continually depressed about what the next day would bring. And yet my gut told me—and my friends told me— that I should keep showing up. My friends convinced me to at least try to work through it. They reminded me of my worth as a teacher. A colleague let me sit in her classroom before school, and she talked with me. I made sure I had breakfast when I didn't want to. I made it through my first lessons, even though they sometimes didn't go very well. There were days when I did, in fact, have panic attacks during class, and I'd lose my words and breath completely and have to excuse myself briefly. I was right—it was scary. In the middle of the day, I tried to get outside and go for walks and talk with friends on the phone, and sometimes meditate.

And I kept teaching. And I taught as well as I could. It seemed like I was counting the hours and days, waiting for it all to pass. In the meantime, I found new healing and support outside of the workplace. Then there were days where I hardly felt anxious at all. I even had some good days. Soon it was the end of the first quarter. I noticed that what I was afraid of was slowly beginning to pass. Things seemed like they were starting to click again. For the most part, I had got through the worst of it.

I've heard people throw around the word *resilience*, but up until then, I didn't know its meaning for me. Resilience to me means taking the action of someone who believes that the worst will pass even when I don't feel like that person. Maybe I didn't *actually* believe that the worst would pass that year, but I took the action anyway. I acted *as if*.

This was not a year I look back on fondly at all. It was absolutely my weakest year in terms of actual teaching. I don't often find myself saying, "I am sure glad I was resilient!" But I am glad I made it through that year. The challenges I've faced since this time, even when unfamiliar, have been much more manageable when I think of that year. Difficult times don't get easier per se, but they are more manageable. I now have my experience as a tool to help me through. And for me, that is a source of great pride.

Reflection: *My actions are one of my greatest tools when I want to grow as a teacher and a person. While thinking and emoting can help me communicate where I am, it is my actions that move me forward. Today I will find ways to use my actions as a strength to help me through a difficult situation or find a solution to something I haven't yet been able to solve.*

On the Physicality of Teaching

Teaching is a surprisingly physical job, and it takes its toll.

On one hand, it is a job that demands so much of our time that caring for ourselves physically is an afterthought. In my first few years of teaching, I came in early and stayed late, and then I'd head home, where I'd work a little more. I could literally feel myself losing muscle mass beneath my teacher clothes.

On the other hand, teaching is a job that requires a great deal from us physically. Now I think I understand why one of my favorite high school teachers had armpit stains on his dress shirts by nine a.m. The type of physical movement we energetic teachers expend isn't the kind of activity that is restorative or strengthening—it takes place under the stress of our constant assistance and awareness, and therefore, it's draining.

My solution for all this at first was to use my summers like rehab to return to my best self, but then August and September would come again, and I'd go back to my unhealthy teaching routine. After only a few years of operating this way, I was exhausted, and it showed. I was living in extremes: push myself to the limit, restore, push myself to the limit, restore . . .

Fortunately, however, my exhaustion arrived at about the time I was also finally beginning to experience one of the promises of sticking around the profession for a while. I was starting to realize that with each teaching year, I had a tiny bit more free time.

There were nights where—gasp!—I didn't take my laptop home. It was then I began peppering in some of the things I'd normally only do in the summer, especially exercise.

And I'm not talking about going out and getting ripped. I'm talking about moving my body in ways that relieve stress, give me some fresh air, and get my system moving.

I started to notice the effect almost immediately. When I'm taking care of my physical health, I feel like I have a little bit more energy for the classroom. I'm also not as exhausted at the end of the school day. Unexpectedly, more energy and physical strength seem to bring with them a source of confidence too. And more confidence, for me, is always a benefit to my interactions in the classroom.

Reflection: *Taking care of myself physically is a way to value my body for my sake, even when I am inclined to make sacrifices to my own care in favor of my work life.*

However, it is good to notice that the ways I take care of myself have a direct effect on how I approach my teaching—when I am restored and healthy, I have more to offer—more energy, strength, and confidence, and far less stress.

On Others' Expectations

Many nights I come home a faint, exhausted version of myself, and I'm not as present as I'd like to be for my loved ones. I find myself relating to the detectives and ER staff on TV dramas whose professions invariably compromise their personal lives.

I've heard it said that teachers often sacrifice their "kids at home" for their "kids at school." On paper, I find this notion problematic, and yet I find myself operating under this belief too. I've been more likely to say, "But my kids need me!" and meant my students at school and not my actual children.

What is driving this? It's a question I've had to look at honestly.

Certainly, I've had students for whom I was fulfilling an essential, urgent role. It made sense that I felt pulled toward them and wanted to give them that extra effort at the expense of my energy and time.

On the other hand, I've experienced the fear that if I wasn't going above and beyond for my students every day, I wasn't a good teacher. This makes a kind of sense too. If you google "inspirational quotes for teachers" right now, you'll find a flood of messaging that we teachers are the ones who are responsible to fix everything wrong with the world. I wonder if much of my effort has been driven by what I think I am *supposed* to be.

I've had to look at the motivations for my efforts squarely to find a balance between my home and school lives that works for me. I stay aware of this balance often, knowing that I've chosen a profession that is particularly taxing and, what's more, can bear the weight of many of society's misplaced expectations for teachers.

Reflection: *When I am honest with myself, I know I spend time and energy that is useful and beneficial to my students and that I also spend time and energy because I am being too hard on myself or I am fearful of how I will be perceived if I don't. Today I will take an honest look at the places in my teaching life that fall into either category and find ways to limit unnecessary work that detracts from other essential pursuits.*

On Honesty About Our Profession

When I began writing this passage, I was afraid to write honestly about my conflicted feelings about our profession, worried that others might not be able to relate. But then I gave it some thought, and I realized I haven't yet met a teacher I've talked with intimately who hasn't acknowledged these feelings to some extent.

Even under the most ideal circumstances—engaged students, supportive parents, and understanding administrators—I have to admit there are times when I've dreaded the job's challenges, was convinced I had nothing left to give, or seriously considered leaving the profession.

And I think it's okay to admit this. Let's look at the facts: some school years, I've calculated that I work ten-to-twelve-hour days and at least a handful of hours on each weekend day. These hours might not be shockingly dissimilar to other professions, but when I consider that teachers in many cases need an advanced degree, have limited avenues for significant financial advancement… not to mention that we are responsible for a minimum of six hours of direct care and enrichment for an entire generation of children; not to mention we are often cast by society in the role of the lazy, money-hungry, unionized ingrates who can't recognize how good they have it (the whole "summers off" argument, etc.) . . . not to mention fear of school violence or feeling the secondhand effects of those who are either exhibiting or asking candidly for help with the symptoms of their very real distress or traumas . . . we have a perfect storm that would wither anyone's will to continue.

It's not all that surprising that these feelings come up. And I think this is important to say.

I think it is also important for me to know that it's okay to feel this way. It's okay if I can't do it. It's okay if I'm burned out and that the job doesn't always give back the way I want it to. It's okay to say it isn't easy and that I sometimes don't like it.

I often read and hear that teachers should be resilient in the face of every challenge. But maybe we shouldn't have to be so resilient for everything and everyone. This job is hard. It can bring me to tears. It can break me. And it can force me to the edge of wanting to leave.

As I write this, I am beginning to notice there is something empowering about getting these feelings out honestly. When I say it's hard, and that I sometimes don't like it, and that in many ways the profession is unfair to the educator, I start to feel something like relief open in me. The pressure valve seems open, much as it does when venting to a friend.

Though I might initially perceive this kind of honesty as "negative" or unshareable because of how it might make me look, I believe that this kind of candidness is affirming and strangely positive. The truth is, I want to understand myself better as an educator. And being honest, even when it's not pretty, is healthier for me than finding ways to cover up the realities of teaching with, say, waves of Twitter-positivity or inspirational memes.

Perhaps being honest about my burnout and the abject difficulties of the profession are ways to protect against giving up. Why? Because, at the end of all this honesty, once I've got all the venting out, I find myself asking this question: "What is it that makes me want to keep doing this anyway?"

And that's when something strange happens. When I ask myself this question, I am slowly filled with the feelings and images of all the times I had a teacher who made learning remarkable for me. These were the teachers who seemed to be making magic in the classroom, who made me feel good about who I was, and who made me feel like I could do what they were doing, or at least that I wanted to try. And somewhere in me, I knew I probably could do it too.

I start to realize what it is I love about this work: the students. I start to see some faces. I see the faces of those who've made me laugh and those who've laughed with me.

I start to feel some hope as I remember how it feels to have that fresh slate of a new school year with new ideas and risks to take and creative ways of making learning work for students. I start to feel a little hope in my job again, even despite all I know to be true. I start to think about how I can make this job work for me within the current realities of education.

I think this hope is the right kind. It isn't longing, and it isn't false. It isn't positive for the sake of being positive. It's a hope born from stating the truth first. And in this way, I start to see a little bit of light.

Reflection: *There is power in honesty. There is power in letting out my real feelings even when they aren't pretty or even when I am scared they are too negative or will reveal something about me that I don't want to look at or let others see. Unexpectedly, however, this honesty can lead to a more balanced understanding of my reality as a teacher. May I trust that being honest with myself—out loud or on paper— is a tool I can use to develop a healthier outlook on myself and my teaching and can lead me to find comfort and hope in the work I do.*

On Education and Social Media

The meeting of education and social media has an immense value for teachers, especially as a resource for lesson ideas and connecting with like minds to share experiences. This has been especially true during the COVID-19 pandemic, as teachers have been able to share best practices about remote learning. However, like every part of the internet, it has its unproductive side.

When I dig too deep into Education Twitter, I mostly experience it the way I experience looking at a feed of people's perfect lives, children, pets, homes, and vacations. I'm left with the feeling that there's no way I'd be able to live up to the standard I'm seeing, or I just *know* in my gut there's more than meets the eye to what's being peddled in 140 characters or a carefully crafted image. These posts on teaching can also feel disorienting when I'm not clear if the motivation is to help teachers and students or to cultivate one's personal brand.

The emergence of "edu-Twitter" can be as agitating as any other part of social media, and it never hurts to look from a distance or find balance in the way I am using it.

It is important for me to be clearheaded and constructive in my engagement with what's shared about teaching online. If I engage during times of stress, I am likely to see other teachers' posts through the lens of unhealthy comparison, envy, or criticism—three very unproductive emotions to carry back to my students.

Reflection: *It's no secret that social media can be toxic, but its best attributes can be life- and world-changing in their ability to inspire the greater good. Today I will look for ways to participate in and draw from ongoing conversations about teaching in a way that I believe will benefit my students and me most.*

On Masks (Or Shells, Etc.)

Most students present themselves to us in their masks: the ways they want to be perceived when they meet someone new. These masks are usually a defense mechanism against a potential threat, something unfamiliar or scary.

Sometimes these masks are recognizable and sweet and easy to like. Think of the student who wants you to know from day one how serious they are about school and how much they want to please you.

But sometimes, these masks are difficult to see past. The student isn't giving you much. And sometimes, the mask is just unpleasant. You feel, as a teacher, that the student is drawing a line in the sand or is telling you to back off. And sometimes, through the mask, they are literally telling you something a little cruder than "back off."

The unpleasant experiences can sting, especially early on when trying to receive the student with enthusiasm about what the year can hold for them.

The conventional teacherly wisdom tells us in these cases to "try to get through to them," "kill them with kindness," or "make a connection." But I'm a little less comfortable these days with the "breakthrough." We use quite a bit of that intrusive language when describing a situation where the student is protecting themselves: *a tough nut to crack*, *get them to come out of their shells*, etc.

Lately, I've been thinking that it might be a good idea to respect the shell first, to give it some integrity, and let it be a while. The shell or the mask (or whatever the metaphor) may exist for any number of reasons and may be as thick as what past hurts our students have faced.

We know we have the talent to help build relationships with students who are resistant to us or to learning, but I think it is important for me to know there are some students whose shells may not break. Some may never take off their masks, and I want to respect this.

For one thing, it's a human right. While we all want better relationships with our students, and while we would all like to serve as a safety net, no one is owed the privilege of a breakthrough, and therefore, I don't necessarily have to achieve this "opening up" to help a student learn or let them know they're cared for.

Teaching usually isn't like the movie where the world-hardened child slowly softens up. Letting an imperfect relationship with a student stay imperfect can still be valuable, for it is a matter of respect; in particular, it is a respect for the student's timetable for how they choose to be. And this, in itself, can be yet another rare and special form of care we teachers can provide.

Reflection: *Difficult or imperfect relationships with our students are always uncomfortable and can bring up our desire to "fix" a situation. There is wisdom, however, in letting these relationships be what they are, not because we are giving up on them, but because we know that time, space, and patience are contributions to a person's development.*

On Meeting the Needs of the Times

Throughout my teaching career, I've noticed that my priorities for my students have shifted to meet the needs of the times.

As workplaces have begun to signal their shift toward reliance on intelligent technology, I've tried to focus on the ways that creativity and human ingenuity can best prepare and differentiate students in a more automated world.

During times of acute political and social crisis, I've felt that media literacy, compassionate listening, and critical thinking about the issues at stake were essential goals.

During the COVID-19 pandemic this past school year, I've focused remote learning on practical skills to establish a sense of consistency and normalcy for my students, collaborative efforts that can connect isolated students, and individualized options that meet the needs of those whose home lives may be in upheaval and who might find flexibility and openness a welcoming, safe gesture in spite of their situation.

I feel very fortunate to have a professional life that is a direct, human, ground-level response to the challenges of our world, and this may be one of the highest rewards of teaching.

Reflection: *One of our unique powers as educators lies in our ability to assist students as they experience the influence—and, sometimes, the shockwaves—of world events. Today I will take up this responsibility with pride and work to meet the specific and often urgent needs of my current students.*

On Responding to Local or National Crises

I know how it feels to have twenty-five students' expectant eyes turned toward me, waiting to hear me speak in the wake of a local or national crisis or tragedy that is on our minds as the school day begins.

I rarely find myself prepared for these occasions. As a teacher, I don't think of myself as an inspiring orator; I'm not gifted at public speaking the way other teachers seem to be.

However, I've found I'm able to meet the needs of my students in these situations by being myself—by being a human being who, like many of us, has to work to find the right words to articulate the depth of my feelings.

I think of a moment, after a great loss in my school's community when I felt almost powerless to speak or act. I stood in the classroom before my students, unmoving, hearing myself breathe, and knowing I should do something, but saying nothing before them; and yet, in that silence, I see now I was telling them wordlessly that it was okay to be present and ineffective and uncertain in our collective and individual grief.

Once this moment passed, I tried to speak from my heart, and it was jumbled and unmemorable, and I did what I could. But my presence and my intent were what mattered there. I could tell then that my students' body language had somewhat eased, knowing I'd created space for the messiness of feeling.

Students need examples of people who are willing to model the various, imperfect, and complex ways we react to the world. That's who I am: imperfect but caring—and I can be effective as I am—even if I'd like to be someone more polished and "inspiring."

It is important to know that I am enough and that who I am makes me an effective teacher, even in our students' most difficult hours. I am the right person to guide my students through times like these and through all times because my personal strengths and instincts are a valid means of caring for students. I'll say this again: the person I am is enough to make me an effective teacher.

Reflection: *My authentic self is a gift to my students. I possess all the qualities they need to be comforted, cared for, and encouraged because these acts are simply a demonstration of who I am. When there is an opportunity to address my students meaningfully, especially in a time of crisis or hurt, I can do so effectively, in the best way I know how without having to become someone I'm not.*

On Violence in Our Schools

Yes, I am afraid of school shootings. Yes, I've imagined how my students and I would escape our classroom. Yes, I've been afraid to come to school in the days following one of these senseless tragedies. I have had to think long and hard about all of this, the reality in which we teachers live.

In so many ways, we are on the front lines: we see poverty, hunger, abuse, discrimination, and illness; but for this kind of violence, I have far less certainty about how to take care of my students who jump from their seats and make concerning eye contact with me at every loud noise in our building.

But here's what I've come up with, and it gives me strength:

First, I let my students know that, yes, I am also afraid—this is scary, yes.

Second, I stay informed. Whether it's running through emergency drills or having the inevitable conversation about school violence in class, I'm prepared to speak consistently, clearly, and calmly about what I know—and what I don't know.

There is power in seeing my students' relief as I demonstrate my humanness ("I'm afraid") and my adult responsibility ("I have given this situation real thought, and I have a plan because I care about you.") All students deserve adults in their lives who can be honest and useful in times of uncertainty. Their relief lets me know that I am doing my part to add something good and loving back to our world as it stands today.

Reflection: *I know there is power in sharing my honest feelings with students, and I know I am capable of providing reassurance through my demeanor as a responsible adult. Today I will find ways to bridge these two strengths and comfort my students' uncertainty or fear with honesty and stability.*

On Teachers and Politics

Whether or not we signed up for it, like it or not, we teachers discover that our profession intersects with the national conversation and, therefore, with politics.

Sometimes it's just noise. We're critiqued in the news and in online comments and social media rants. We are what ails society or what cures it. We are the target of the public's anger, or we are the heroes. One election season, it's educational reforms. Next time around, they want to forgive us our loans and pay us more. Again, mostly noise.

But in this new decade, it's been difficult to ignore the voices of teachers. We have found ourselves playing a necessary role in our country's most important issues: systemic racism, economic inequality, the COVID-19 pandemic, and gun regulation—to name the most significant. It seems our job touches all parts of American life—and its wounds.

It is clear that the perspectives of teachers can't be counted out as a significant force in the healing of our country. And that's because we are powerful. And we are powerful because we are necessary, vital. Many hopes are hinged on what we can do with our talents and experience.

This role was an unexpected addition to my job description when I started my career. But I suppose it shouldn't have been so surprising after all; there aren't many other professions that have personal, essential, consequential contact with such a broad swath of the population.

I see this as a blessing. It is encouraging to know my work in the classroom, making a daily contribution to the well-being and education of my students, is an act of meaningful participation in the health and growth of our society. And further, it is comforting to know my work will never feel absent of a larger purpose.

Reflection: *To know we have a career that intersects with the most important issues of our day is not something everyone can claim. And yet, this does not mean that we must take up the entire mantle of solving society's ills. Today I will recognize my own power, vitality, and essentiality as an educator and continue to fill this role in practical, manageable ways.*

On My Identity and Classroom Culture

When I think about the white American male teacher's appearances in the media, the caricatures are frustratingly easy to imagine. He's either the hypermasculine jackass with a whistle, a creep, or a sensitive romantic in tweed who is far too invested in his students' personal lives. And I'm pretty sure that's about it.

You have to wonder how these caricatures play into the ways students expect me to behave as a teacher, as someone whose racial and gender identity matches the one above.

We know that this identity has had, and continues to have, its many toxic iterations since time immemorial, and teachers I've encountered over the years who identify similarly certainly aren't making it any easier.

Here's a quick example: I once overheard a white male teacher in his classroom commenting on a video clip of a white actress, a person whose body was often discussed in popular media. The teacher was repeatedly and laughingly referring to her as his "future wife." I had to wonder what his students were learning from this joke and what they were learning about this teacher whom they were asked to trust. And what this teacher was really communicating to them. And what was being established about the kind of behavior that is permissible. This is just one example of the casual, supposedly inoffensive stuff that happens daily in American classrooms.

In my own classroom, I've noticed there are three common personal questions I am asked by students every year without fail—questions that seem largely wrapped up in stereotypes and assumptions about me. The questions are, in order: 1) what sports did you play in high school? 2) did you go to prom? and 3) did you go with your girlfriend?

From all this, I think it is safe to conclude that students have a limited view of who I can be to them and what to expect from me. And I think this adds up to one thing: there's some work to be done.

Because of my place at center stage when students are in my classroom, I've come to recognize there's an opportunity to demonstrate my healthy, individual, nuanced self that does not quite match their expectations, and which, for students who are often consuming caricatures and biased views of various identities, and who are, importantly, involved in the long process of understanding themselves—can be surprisingly educational.

I can also establish a classroom culture in which our society's biases and assumptions are shut down, debunked, and subverted, not promoted or idealized. I feel that one easy starting point in creating this culture is to look at my own behavior—to consider what messages are being transmitted to my students through my behavior.

What am I communicating? What am I allowing to be said or not said? And here's a tough one: am I prepared to sacrifice a connection with a student, or am I ready to give up gaining some form of "credibility" when I decide to speak up against problematic notions? Am I ready to unpack and disarm these notions to defend healthier ones with tact and respect?

Being able to consider these questions has become another enriching contribution I can make to the lives of my students. This work has added an extra layer of purpose and pride to my teaching and has even reinforced the person I am outside the classroom too. The kind of model I want to be for my students is in direct relation to the kind of person I strive to be in the world at large.

Today, as a teacher, I not only get to care about how my students learn, but I also get to carry with me and demonstrate an example of adulthood that reveals all I've learned about how I see myself, how I view and relate to others, and how I continue to grow.

Reflection: *My way of being in the world can be an example to students and can, in some cases, serve to complicate or counteract more problematic notions in the culture at large. Today, I will observe the ways I contribute to and ultimately establish a classroom culture that offers more than assumptions, expectations, stereotypes, and caricatures. I will notice and try to strengthen the ways I can successfully model more layered, loving, open-minded, and open-hearted ways of being in the world.*

On Ways of Listening

Many of our students' struggles are right in front of our faces, but there are other students who are also struggling as learners or in their personal lives and are not particularly vocal or demonstrative about the difficulties they're facing.

For these students, we must be able to understand the various ways they communicate their needs, which sometimes come out sideways, or faintly, or in code.

We have to be very aware and awake to take care of these kinds of students. Despite the special intuition we teachers possess, I admit I've occasionally missed the signs, and the chances, to help a student in need.

I want to continue to refine my skills as a listener and observer of my students so I can hear their voices, even those who speak softest.

Reflection: *I still remember those adults in my life who listened to me as a younger person and the impact that simple action had on me. I will remember today that listening can be a radical act that empowers others and that listening is a muscle that can be strengthened with practice. I will look for the softest voice and give it space in my life.*

On Being a Teacher-Ally in the Fight Against Hatred

All too often, I hear my students share their horrifying experiences with direct acts of racism, sexism, homophobia, transphobia, xenophobia, Islamophobia, antisemitism, ableism, and the myriad ugly forms of prejudice, discrimination, and hatred.

It is especially urgent for me to care for those who are hurting with an ever-evolving plan, knowing that the ways I respond as an adult can either assist in setting students on a path to healing or further exacerbate the harm that has been done.

Understanding that I must have this plan at the ready is part of the role of the teacher-ally, a role I believe should be at the top of all teachers' job descriptions.

I must commit to a continuous habit of educating myself about the larger and smaller acts of aggression or discrimination that people, particularly those who are marginalized, experience on a day-to-day basis. This requires listening, reading, learning, seeking, and empathizing—so that I know what to look and listen for.

I need to be well-read in what national, state, and local resources are available to students who have been harmed because of these acts, and I need to know which qualified professionals to turn to.

I must pay attention to local and national events, including news stories and legislation, as these instances can often be sources of distress or uncertainty for certain students.

And most importantly, in all of this work, I must keep my students' specific needs in mind. I need to understand, respect, and honor the various ways that individuals want to be approached, listened to, and supported.

In short, I need to be well versed, prepared, and responsive—all of which are forms of love and care.

I can never settle for less than a clear, actionable plan for my students, especially as these forms of hatred continue to poison our culture daily. I may be okay with the occasional weak lesson plan, but I am never okay with failing to enact the radical listening, precision, and compassion required of me when seeking to help those who have been affected by these unconscionable acts.

Reflection: *Allyship as a teacher is a serious and important role. It requires learning, listening, and specific action. It is possible I am the first, or only, adult to discover that a student has been harmed by acts of prejudice and hatred. Today I will reaffirm the distinctive role I play in defending my students' humanity.*

On Our Chance to See the Future

One of my favorite brags about being a teacher is that I can speak authentically—and proudly— about the current generation of young people who are being educated in our schools.

As it happens, I now have experience teaching two generations of students, and I can say with certainty that each has given me hope. By interacting closely with my students, I get to watch in real time how our society has influenced our students; but even more significantly, it becomes clear to me how the next generation of adults will likely shape our society themselves.

Are high school bathrooms still gross? Yep. Do kids still do things that are just as hurtful, get into the same types of trouble, and find ways to frustrate the hell out of all the rest of us? Yes.

And aren't our children just inheriting a world that might shape them toward its desires before they can shape the world to theirs? Maybe.

But it's easy to be a cynic.

I like trying to see what they're doing right. And I think they're doing a lot right.

I love their dedication to social issues. I love their dedication to justice. I love their sense of humor and creativity and ingenuity. I love that they know there are more paths to success than the traditional ones I was raised on. I love that their art is more inclusive. I love that they are more inclusive. I love that they are critical. And radical. It's not just a pose.

Not many professions have the privilege of watching the world change. It is only a very small number of us who get to contribute to the lives of those who are about to take the helm.

I count this experience as one of the many blessings of my career. I get to watch and witness at the ground level as the present moment of humanity flows ever forward.

Reflection: *When I step back from my day-to-day teaching, there are many aspects of my career that are exceptional but that I don't often consider. Today I will purposefully divert my attention from my to-do lists and tasks to notice the overlooked aspects of being a teacher that bring me a sense of pride about the work I do.*

On Protecting Students from My Stress

We all know the expression about what rolls downhill, and most teachers understand this well. How many times in my career have I felt my job would be everything I ever wanted it to be if all it entailed was me, my ideas and lessons, and a willingness to do whatever I can for my students?

Unfortunately, I don't think I've had a year in my profession in which new technology and new initiatives or mandates haven't frustrated my plans for students or raised my stress level significantly.

However, I feel there is an ethics in our profession that says no matter how complicated or baffling these situations can be, we can't let this stress go further than us.

Why? Because that's where our students are. We teachers are in place to shield our students from institutional difficulties as best we can—we who must receive these difficulties, then turn around, close our doors, and do what's best for our students. Children are sponges for dysfunction in our other social institutions (marriage, anyone?), and they are equally perceptive about and susceptible to the free-floating stressors of education as well.

So what kind of model will I be on the hill of a system I think is in need of reform? If I choose to be critical of this system, I can model this stance with maturity and discretion, a teachable moment. Like many of us, however, if I choose to accept things as they are, it's unfair to bring my students into it. Admittedly, I've done this in the past with eye rolls and sly comments and irritability in front of my students. But these behaviors are merely passive-aggressive outlets for my stress, which needs to be resolved elsewhere.

Part of contributing to the emotional health of my students—which is absolutely essential for learning—is to find a way to teach them within the system at play. And what can students really do with the conflicting message that the "system is broken" but that these are supposed to be the best years of their lives?

Reflection: *Even when the challenges of the profession affect me negatively, I can learn to manage my stress by owning it and finding the proper channels for release. In this way, I can say I am thoroughly committed to doing what's best for my students. May I recognize that how I face difficulties in front of my students is, in fact, a far healthier model for them than wishing conditions were exactly how I want them.*

On Superheroes

The old "it was weird seeing my teacher in the grocery store" story says a lot about the fact that, yes, teachers are larger than life. And, yes, "all we do" is hard to imagine. But the whole "teachers are superheroes" thing is, for me, a little more complicated.

An example: one school year, I was excited about the idea of individualizing my instruction to each of my students' needs. I imagined a class full of conferences and experimentation with each student. I was sure this would work, and I was ready to take the risk.

That August, however, I started looking at my rosters. Each day they seemed to grow. Soon I was borrowing extra desks. Then I was giving up my own desk. Then I was making the radiator comfy. My class sizes didn't seem to invite the kind of exploratory approach I'd imagined.

And that's when I was about to do something all too familiar and safe for me: I was about to tie on that "teachers are superheroes" cape to embark on one of those foolhardy errands where I fly through the hallways saying, *I'm going to do this anyway! I am going to make this work! That's what teachers do: we take what's given to us, and we turn it into gold. We are here FOR THE KIDS!!!*

I was about to give up my free time, sleep, relationships, health, and well-being to manage and squeeze and will my way into realizing my plans as if all of that unmanageable effort in spite of impossible conditions automatically equated to guaranteed student learning.

I always have to question myself when I say "for the kids." If I'm being honest, I was spending a lot of time thinking about how I'd look "for the kids" *and the adults* as I made these sacrifices. You know, "Teacher of the Year" material. So was it really for the kids after all?

I've responded to the call of the superhero so many times that it's easy to think this way. We teachers might argue that this type of thinking is encouraged and rewarded. We might argue that the superhero thing was created so teachers can run themselves ragged for the things they need, like funding and support, while they forget about the real causes of their school's lack of resources.

This time around, however, I decided not to do it. This time I felt like things weren't right. I got that feeling I get sometimes when I am trying to make something, anything, work that I know isn't going to work without contorting the mind and spirit. Maybe it's because I'd already exhausted myself with this way of thinking throughout my career, and now I was ready to make a change.

It occurred to me then that every time I take on the mantle of sacrifice and stress, I am caught up in an illusion I've created for myself. But these class sizes weren't my fault! I didn't need to make up for that! I'm not the one who created these circumstances. I don't have to clean up the mess. I am going to do okay. It isn't what I'd planned, but I still know I'm going to be okay.

The truth is, a teacher can do great things for kids without trying to wriggle out of the conditions imposed by the educational system itself, in this case, my unwieldy class sizes. The good news is I can bend over backward for my students, sure, but I don't have to break in half.

And though it was uncomfortable, and I often felt I had to justify my approach to my teacher friends why I was teaching so "traditionally" that year (as if I owed them some sort of confession), it ended up being a very good year.

I think of it this way: it's not as if my former students are writing me all the time to tell me how life-changing and grand that year was when I went that totally stress-driven, self-driven extra mile for some convoluted and untenable plan. No. The trickle of emails and cards come in from the self-made "superhero" years and my more balanced years just the same. Being human and less "super" can work just fine for me.

Reflection: *I have to be honest about what I can and can't do as a teacher. This requires looking at a situation clearly to decide what kind of efforts need to be made versus efforts that are not healthy choices for me. For us teachers who dream big and want the best for our students, this can be difficult to see clearly. However, I can practice finding ways to work with challenges of the profession instead of against them, knowing I can do so with strength, creativity, care, and success.*

On Understanding Parents and Guardians

I've noticed that frustration is an emotion that often comes out sideways: I am likely to express it in ways that do not directly confront what I'm upset about.

I've noticed this phenomenon, too, when working with parents and caretakers in high-intensity situations. Sometimes a parent will be upset with me, or short, or rude, and I react in kind.

When I'm reacting like this, whatever the solution is— whatever care or assistance the student needs—is limited by this reaction, and I'm breeding more conflict.

So I've had to learn how to handle stressful interactions with parents and caretakers to do my job well. When I start to understand that parents' and caretakers' frustrations are likely not personal and are probably just as misdirected as my own frustrations can be, these moments become a whole lot easier to handle.

I've learned that it's more often the case that parents are experiencing very human and very normal emotions: they are concerned for their child in some way, uncertain about how they are being perceived as a parent, afraid they've made a wrong choice about their child's schooling, or perhaps there is some other issue that has taken place in the past that has snowballed into the feelings that are being demonstrated here in the present, even if it's aimed at the wrong person.

Understanding this truth about my feelings and being able to see them for what they are allow me to be far more forgiving and far more able to move past my reactions to the unpleasant emotions of a parent. When I can act on this understanding, I'm more capable of making sure the reason we've come together is addressed effectively and with more compassion.

Reflection: *There are so many opportunities in our day to see past the immediate behavior of a student, colleague, or parent in order to recognize their deeper human needs. May I have the insight to see beyond both my reactions and theirs, that I might be compassionate while protecting myself from emotions within me I'd rather not bring to the table.*

On Working Well with Administrators and Supervisors

Tension can easily arise between teachers and their administrators for a very simple and understandable reason.

Our profession's primary relationship is not one between employees and bosses, but teachers and students, and far more rarely than in other professions do teachers have to report directly to a supervisor regarding the specifics of their day-to-day work in the classroom.

Most of the art of teaching is handled between a teacher and their classes with the support of the teachers around us, and this is primarily where our energy goes.

Therefore, there can be a great deal of misunderstanding, especially from teachers, who feel, because we have autonomy over our classroom time, that administrators are asking for things we believe are out of touch with the nuanced and complex efforts of teaching. And this is entirely understandable.

My error, however, is that I can mistake the authority I have over my own classroom for a kind of overall autonomy and freedom without the typical accountability that governs other professions.

But the truth is that even without direct oversight, discovering the benefits and rewards of working within the constraints of what I am being expected to do is the adult and professional way of seeking freedom and creative license in the classroom.

Otherwise, our frustrations end up with no place for release but in gossip and complaint, or, worse, they end up on the shoulders of our students. I am entirely guilty of both reactions. But neither impulse has made me feel like I truly won anything back, and I feel even less satisfied with my work than ever.

This is not to say that we shouldn't collaborate with and, yes, respectfully critique the decisions of our supervisors or work to ensure that these decisions are reasonable and equitable, for efforts of healthy communication are essential to the overall well-being of a school, its leaders, teachers, and students.

And yet I try to be mindful that even when I have strong beliefs about what is best for my students, and even when I feel empowered by my place as a highly knowledgeable source of information about student learning (because that can be the truth), it serves me well, and it serves the stability and happiness of my career well, to understand and occupy my role as a teacher working in tandem with others who, we have to remember, got into this profession because they also know the rewards of teaching well.

Reflection: *We teachers want to feel supported by our leaders, and, also, because of our knowledge and experience, we want the freedom to do what is best for our students. May I have the wisdom to advocate for myself in this way, as well as work to healthily, thoughtfully address the needs of my school's leadership.*

On Observations and Evaluations

I've never liked having my classes observed and evaluated. Even when it all goes well, I've never felt comfortable with the fact that I've just put on a performance. I don't like feeling self-conscious in front of my students, and to me, there's always been something a little troubling about having to shift to the role of the evaluated employee in the very space and culture I've created for my students.

I guess, in short, I've never liked playing the game. But guess what? No one does, and yet there's always a game to play. These systems and interactions are common in any workplace, but maybe we teachers are a little more sensitive, given that what we're doing daily is carefully and artfully building then balancing a house of cards we know in advance will topple, only to build it back up again. To be evaluated at any random point in this ongoing tenuous and shaky process feels a little inaccurate as a measure of our ability.

However, as someone who has dreaded observations and evaluations for years, I've discovered one way to approach this necessary part of our jobs that takes a little of its difficulty and strangeness away and makes the process more meaningful for me as a teacher and professional.

The key for me is to invite my evaluator in as a collaborator and ask them to work with me on understanding specific parts of my teaching that I know aren't successful. We teachers are always thinking about making improvements to our work, so why not offer an honest question as a lens through which to see our classroom? Honesty and openness go a long way, and I often feel much more at ease with higher-ups when I can break the ice about the actual challenges I am facing as opposed to hiding these things through some deft performance.

I also like to be able to guide the narrative about what I hope my evaluator will focus on. This is empowering for me too. If I can establish in advance what both the evaluator and I are there to witness, and if I've been genuine about what I want to work on, I can get into the mindset that we are teammates trying to find the best way to benefit *our* students as opposed to this being an opportunity to evaluate my teaching wholesale. Focusing on students is something that energizes both administrators and teachers, so this approach feels right.

Reflection: *Teaching can produce a great deal of discomfort and anxiety in our lives, even as we know its highs and rewards. However, we can focus on both honest communication and what we can control as methods to empower ourselves during these difficult moments. Today I will consider how the principles of openness and self-initiative can make a difference for me in my teaching.*

On Parent-/Caretaker-Teacher Conferences

I didn't fully understand what it meant to interact
with my students' parents and caretakers until I became
a parent, until it was my turn to sit on the *other side*
of the desk for a parent-teacher conference about my
own children.

As a teacher, I tend to find these meetings tiresome.
I've often quipped that the caretakers who show up are
the ones whose students need the least amount of help,
or I find myself frustrated and quick to judge them for
enacting the same kind of difficulties in the conference as
their students have in the classroom. This thinking seems
to be a default mode for me, and I'm not proud of it.

I need to be honest about what's behind this cynicism.
What's behind it, for me, is that I am, in a misdirected way,
being hypercritical of conferencing because there's fear
involved. Sure, conference time can be a long and arduous
part of the year, but I think what's really happening is
that I'm afraid of being surprised by a worst-case scenario,
that a conference will go off the rails and I'm suddenly
cornered and called out because my teaching isn't working,
and I have no articulate defense.

Each school year seems to be another grand
experiment as I try on new ideas and new ways of helping

students, and sometimes I just don't have the perfect answer that justifies my methods. Not having that answer while face to face with a parent can be scary.

And so I create these little dramas in my head where I'm superior and above these conferences to protect myself. It's nonsense. I need to remember what's essential about these meetings. Yes, there might be some day-to-day drama to discuss and some solutions and strategies for improvement, but I also need to think about what I've discovered as a parent and recent attendee at these meetings.

What I really want to hear from a teacher is that my child is cared for—that they are special and significant. I want to know that my child has gone out into the world and has been discovered as someone who can be loved and seen for who they are. Parents want to hear what they already know to be true echoed back to them. It's just like in the classroom: I can have great plans and solutions and strategies, but sometimes I forget that children (and their parents) just want to be noticed, discovered, and praised.

This is a gift I can bring to any conference, no matter how contentious or arduous they might be and no matter how critical or fearful my default mode might be. To arm myself with care and respect and kindness for a child or parent always seems to make the burdensome parts of my job lighter again and the challenges more meaningful.

Reflection: *It is important for me to bring my work back to its basics: my ability to notice and praise the strengths of my students. Today I will find ways to engage with this work of uplifting my students so that I do not get carried away by the negativity, fear, or cynicism that often comes with the work-a-day life of the teacher.*

On Clashing with Students

There are students I've just not been able to connect with. While I pride myself on building good relationships, I've had my share of those who were disinterested in engaging with me when they arrived and were disinterested on the way out.

Looking back on past relationships like these, there wasn't much I could have done to make them better, regardless of what I tried, and, of course, I tried everything I could think of.

While these situations are occurring, however, I experience a great deal of discomfort and can often feel these students' presence weighing on me while I'm teaching; therefore, I've found it necessary to better understand why I feel this way.

Teaching is a collaborative act of give-and-take between my students and me, and I measure a lesson's success by my students' reactions and feedback, so it's natural to feel uneasy when a student isn't having it.

And yet, I've also had to consider that perhaps my level of discomfort is more about desiring perfection from my students as well as my internalized expectations about what a classroom is supposed to look like. I can get caught up with the idea that I'm surely behaving in some way that is unlikable to that student, or I feel I'm abdicating my responsibility to engage all students or failing to do some necessary work that would improve the relationship.

The reality of our world, however, is that there are sometimes people we simply aren't able to connect with, and to expect otherwise is telling ourselves that this reality isn't true for teachers. The perfect lessons, classes, and students are just not consistently available to even the best of us.

Some lessons fail, and there are students we're unable to reach. Is this encouraging? No. But looking honestly and practically at these situations seems to provide a little more freedom and comfort: I can be more gentle with myself, feel more at ease with my concerns, and even make more natural and less fraught efforts to work alongside all of my students, no matter their reactions.

Reflection: *Understanding that I am simply a human being in a room with other human beings is a practical reminder that the dynamics of the world at large can just as easily occur in a classroom, including the experience of conflict and disharmony. May I continue to look honestly at my expectations for students as well as continue to develop new ways of seeing myself as a teacher.*

On Apologies

There are things I've regretted saying to students. I've been harsher than I needed to be. I've been angry. I've misread situations. I've been quick with a retort. I've spoken too soon. These instances are not the norm, but I still remember them well. I wonder if my students do too.

In each case, a basic theme is present: I felt embarrassed, disrespected, or afraid in some way, and I didn't give myself time to get my feelings out of the way to think and reflect and listen before saying something in the moment.

And in each case, regardless of whether there was fault on the part of the student, I owed an apology.

I have never regretted apologizing to a student, even when the student claims to have forgotten the offense. I can still tell when we're face to face, that my effort is meaningful to them.

At the very least, an apology, when warranted, can be an important demonstration of my integrity and what it looks like to do the right, necessary thing. It is a way of showing my students that, as an adult with some degree of power in the classroom, I am committed to using that power responsibly and for their benefit.

Most importantly, recognizing where I fall short and making amends show my students that I am invested in and care about how we interact, which is ultimately what I think a good apology is about.

Reflection: *Effective apologies and attempts to make peace have had a great effect on me. They defuse tension, forge a deeper connection, and demonstrate one's generosity of spirit, empathy, and thoughtfulness. Today I will be aware of the ways I can have this effect on my students through my actions.*

On Difficult Students

Whenever I hear about students changing for the better, I think of "J." Though J. had been a disruptive force in my classroom because of her obvious and vocal distaste for my teaching—not to mention her keen ability to direct everyone's attention toward her at all times—I was shocked when I ran into her a few years later.

She was excited to talk to me. She thanked me for all of my help, which left me scratching my head. She wanted me to read a paper she'd written that she was very proud of. And I *was* very, very proud of her—but also puzzled. J. seemed to have had a very different experience in my class than I'd had. And yet, I was thrilled to see the change in her.

Now, whenever I have a new student whose actions remind me of J.'s, I feel a kind of lightness where before there was only tension. Sure, I'm also still preparing myself for what difficulties might occur, but thanks to J., I feel far more patient, accepting, and even a little bit happy knowing I can weather the challenges ahead with far more kindness now that I'm aware of what can become of my students down the road.

Reflection: *I always welcome a chance to see my students in a new light, knowing that this will relieve some of my anxiety about our interactions, make me feel more connected to them, and help me find ways to teach them more effectively. Today I will try to see a student more clearly and openly in hope that this will benefit our interactions.*

On the Anxious Student

I am thinking today about the anxious, bright student who wants to get everything right. They want a good grade, a perfect score, and the reassurance that they are excellent.

When I first started teaching, I was afraid of these students because they can often be confrontational. I was afraid they would say something critical about me or question my teaching in a way I didn't know how to defend. There were times where I would try to avoid them or write them off as being disrespectful.

And I can still feel that way.

Except now, with experience, I know that it's important for me to begin my relationship with these students knowing more about where their feelings are coming from. This looks different for each individual, but it likely includes collaboration with parents, counselors, and other teachers. It may include getting to know the student in a less emotionally charged setting.

Whether their anxiety derives from their home environment, their giftedness, a neurodivergence, or another stressor, it is important for me to do the work to understand that it's not personal.

As a result, I am better prepared to receive these students' stress without fear, and, more importantly, I can be helpful and useful to these students who need nurturing, not more conflict.

Reflection: *Students do not interact with their teachers without context. Their family lives, experiences, challenges, and strengths all play roles in how they interact with us. Today I will look for opportunities to expand my understanding of where my students are coming from. I will remember that this understanding will help me to support them more effectively, and it gives my students the space they deserve to be themselves, just as they are.*

On Difficult Classes

We've all had that one class, or—at the very least—that one day. I've had both. More than once.

I've spent full semesters with classes I couldn't keep on track for anything. Most of the students refused my assistance and directions, earned Cs, Ds, and Fs exclusively, and their various challenges were so difficult to manage that I would start to get more and more anxious as the clock crept closer to class time.

I've also had single class periods that, when they ended, found me with my forehead on my desk trying not to cry out of pure embarrassment at my lack of classroom management.

I'd like to say that I can now write these classes off as early learning experiences as I ascended the rungs toward my life as a veteran teacher; if I'm honest, though, my most out-of-control class was in year nine, and the last memory I have of a class period that really pained me in a lasting way was definitely in the past couple of years.

But if you're a new teacher, take heart! Truly. It's okay to have classes and days like this. They happen to us all, even the veterans. These experiences even happen to folks I consider the very best classroom teachers I've ever seen. These challenging classes are usually the exception, though, and not the rule. I've gone years without either a wildly difficult class or too many truly rough days. I've also improved my ability to handle these situations when they do come up, even the ones that have occurred further into my teaching career than I'd like to admit.

The most important thing for me to remember is that these classes are *not* a reflection of my ability as a teacher but an intersection of various dynamics that are often out of my control. I can see this in hindsight, but when I was in the middle of it, I felt like it was my responsibility to clean up the mess, so it didn't look like I was clueless.

I now know that it's okay for things to not go as planned. It's okay to try new techniques, strategies, and approaches week to week—that's how we build experience. It's also okay to get others involved when we feel lost. There are trusted teacher friends and mentors who can assist, and administrators can be strong and understanding supports when we throw our hands in the air. It's also okay to make changes when we don't feel we are being supported; our profession has many avenues and opportunities, and the right fit for each of us is out there. I know this from experience, and I've seen it happen for others.

I am here to tell you that difficult classes are survivable. As I sit here writing this, I am happy to be a teacher who only has a passing memory of these events.

I have to remember that teaching a classroom of students is a lot like juggling plates: twenty-five of them (on average) after a night of insufficient sleep and having performed this plate routine several other times that day. It's okay to go easy on ourselves. These days, and these classes, most definitely pass.

Reflection: *Teaching can sometimes give us more than we can handle, and it is fine to feel overwhelmed, as it is an experience we share with all educators. May I be able to weather my most difficult moments with courage and the understanding that these experiences are truly temporary.*

On Emulating the Greats

There are a few teachers I've had in my life whose mannerisms and personalities in class were so appealing that I wanted to be just like them when I one day had my own classroom.

Some of these teachers were soft-spoken but piercingly kind and present; others had bombast, were hilarious, and made us feel their electricity. And each were so consistent in the roles they played for us that we looked forward to their familiarity and comfort.

When I started teaching in my own classroom, and no one was around but my students, I started to try on some of these great teachers' signature quips and jokes and mannerisms, and even their voices. In a way, I was sort of channeling my favorite teachers for my students, hoping that some of the joy I experienced in learning from the greats would transfer to my own students.

It was a little weird, maybe. But I think everybody must do this to some degree (. . . right?) These were the teachers who made me want to try my hand at teaching. These were the ones who made it feel like a pleasure to learn, who reminded me that learning could be a kind of entertainment.

I think this was an important part of my development: to emulate and even imitate the teachers I thought were exceptional. All I was really saying was I want to be like them, and maybe I can make myself like them.

In order to get good at something, we want our students to follow directions and procedures that lead to success. We want them to imitate the habits of those who have been successful before them. Artists do this, of course, and the same thing goes for teaching, also an art form.

Trying to be like the teachers I admired gave me some comfort and protection as well as an identity when I was new and felt like I didn't have much to offer.

And then I woke up one day, and I was just a teacher in the middle of teaching a class. It suddenly occurred to me that I was simply doing my thing; I was no longer "trying." I could see myself from the outside doing my job, and naturally. I am glad I found my way into the role. And I feel proud that I accomplished this by taking the risk of following, resembling, and imitating, all to ultimately become myself.

Reflection: *"Acting as if" is time-honored wisdom and can be applied in larger ways, like becoming a teacher, and in smaller everyday ways, like doing something new for the first time or pushing through difficult feelings. It's okay to try on a self that isn't "us" for a while, for it can serve as confidence and extra courage when we need it.*

On the Power of Mentors

I've had two very important mentors in my teaching life. One of them was assigned to me, and the other I naturally gravitated toward, an experience I know many young teachers have.

One of the things I love best about them was that they both genuinely saw me as someone with potential. I still admire their ability to see beyond my first-year challenges, and they seemed to really care about my journey as a teacher. They found humor in my youthful thinking and anxieties, and they also made me feel good about my early successes. They were unconcerned when I was convinced I'd completely blown it, and in one case, my first mentor covered for me when I made the inevitable mistakes we new teachers make.

There is a meditation practice in a certain school of Buddhism in which the meditator imagines the people who love and care for them most, encircling the meditator and sending beams of love, benevolence, kindness, light—any kind of love the meditator can imagine.

When I am down about my teaching, I still rely on the wisdom and kindnesses and love of my mentors. What they gave me then was unconditional. They saw me at my most raw and vulnerable. If someone produced a recording of my teaching efforts from that time, I'd quickly want it deleted, but my mentors chose to accept me as I was and helped me find ways to improve. They made me feel a part of their team, gave me shout-outs when I was thriving, and pep-talked me into trying it all again tomorrow. I am sure my successes today are grounded in their early work with me, and I find comfort in revisiting their words and actions when I'm in need.

Reflection: *Our mentors believe in us as teachers, and this is a gift. There is something significant about having an experienced teacher—one who understands what it's like—encourage us at our most difficult hour. Today I will recognize and feel the care of these mentors and see in myself what these mentors have seen in me. I will remind myself that there are always people in my life who are willing to be there to support me, even when I'm not at my best.*

On New-Teacher Guardedness

I decided to become a teacher and fell in love with teaching because of the joy I experienced when helping students achieve what they weren't sure they could achieve— and yet I entered my first days of teaching nervously and with a single hope: don't let them get the best of you.

Reinforced by the silly "don't smile until Christmas" rule, the admonishments of veteran teachers, and some natural, normal first-year jitters, I suddenly found myself more anxious than excited about my work. The number of mental gymnastics and strategizing I did to steel myself against all possible student misbehavior felt overwhelming at times.

I ran into as many situations where I assumed my students were trying to dupe me or disrespect me as instances of actual disrespect (though there was, of course, some—which is also normal!), and I interpreted a great deal of student behavior as a direct "threat" to my classroom when it wasn't. Also, shamefully, I noticed myself assuming certain students were out to rattle me while convincing myself of the integrity of others. I was guarded—very guarded—and it showed.

I never liked these feelings, and I still don't like them when they pop up now. The good news is they're not some inherent flaw of mine as a teacher—it can all be learned from and changed.

We should remember there's so much we want to go right: we want our students to learn, and we want them to be willing enough to get there. We aren't sure if our students are going to trust us and accept us as someone who can help them and make them feel smart and capable, which all students want, regardless of the different ways it might take to get there. It makes sense that we'd lack confidence and exhibit this in ways we'd prefer not to, out of fear.

New teachers, again, take heart! As I've grown into this job, I've found that one of the certain promises of sticking around is that we soon let our guard down. The personas we've created to gain respect becomes unnecessary, and student behavior becomes a secondary concern.

It all happens as we learn how to practice and demonstrate what is really inside us, what we're most capable of as teachers, and what we do best: our commitment and preparedness, our genuine willingness to help our students, and our belief they can all rise to high expectations.

When we work on this, things start to look up. Students come around. They trust us more, and we trust them (mostly). We learn we don't need to protect against less pleasant forms of student behavior when they do crop up. And the joy and creativity, naturalness, and ease that marked our reasons for becoming teachers in the first place return. From one teacher to another: it's a fact.

Reflection: *Being guarded as a teacher is a normal reaction to the nature of our profession. It is okay to feel these feelings. But it is also good to know that we can grow out of these feelings. Today I will keep my focus on doing what teachers do best with an eye toward the ways my work will ultimately transform my classroom and teaching experience.*

On Friendships with Colleagues

One of the best ways to relieve the stress of our jobs as educators is perhaps an obvious one—our social connections with those who understand us well: other teachers.

For those who are new to the profession, these friendships are one of a kind. There's nothing quite like sharing the burden of stress with each other. Our colleagues are exhausted, too, and are experiencing the same difficulties we are. They understand. They get it. Our teacher friends are encountering the same absurdities that come with our profession, too, and these are best endured with laughter.

Whenever we vent or complain or swap stories with each other, we are, in effect, imagining ourselves in each other's shoes, and this happens easily and naturally because we likely have a story or two to match their own. In these moments, we can find a great deal of comfort, either as the storyteller or the listener.

These relationships need not be built exclusively with folks we're likely to socialize with outside of school. The common bond we teachers have with each other can sometimes supersede our tastes and beliefs. I've made some unlikely friendships in my teaching life because of our common experiences. I'm thankful for this, for I may not have had the opportunity otherwise.

There is another profound effect that comes from our relationships with colleagues. When someone shares a story with me that I haven't yet experienced myself, I listen more closely now because I've discovered how likely it is that I will face that challenge someday.

And when I do finally find myself in their shoes, I am more likely to catch myself before getting overwhelmed because I know someone else has already been through the experience and shared it with me and came out on the other side okay. This lightens the burden of a stressful situation, and in these moments, I can almost feel the presence of my teacher friend there with me.

To know I am not alone and that an empathetic ear is waiting when the bell rings can lessen the weight of whatever I'm experiencing.

Reflection: *One of the rewards of teaching is that we are surrounded by so many others who understand the profession. Our storytelling is a powerful way of alleviating stress for each other and forging lifelong friendships built from a common bond and commitment to teaching. May I continue to foster these relationships to care for my colleagues and myself.*

On the Sick Day

I've heard it said that it's harder to have a sick day than it is to be in school. I know the feeling. The school day has to function without us, but without us, there's plenty that can go wrong. We find ourselves, instead of resting, coaching a substitute through technology issues, helping them handle difficult students, and interpreting lesson plans for them while keeping up on our emails. We start to deprioritize the very thing we took a sick day to prioritize: ourselves.

This scenario makes sick and personal days into decisions I wrestle with more than I should, and I know other teachers feel similarly. I notice how many of my colleagues come to school when they're ill. Once, when my car died, I walked along the highway in the rain soaked up to my ankles while carrying my little canvas lunch bag to catch an Uber from a gas station because I wanted to be present for a lesson I thought was important.

Here's the key to unlocking the truth in this scenario: I *thought* the lesson was important. I don't even remember what the lesson was about now. My students from that school year have no advantage over others in their adult lives today because I was able to make it in on time with wet socks. I could have stayed in my car and come in late.

I sit here now thinking about all the times I've done something like the car incident out of a need to ensure order. If I dig deeper, however, it was really because I was worried someone would think I wasn't dedicated or that my students would "talk." This is the least desirable side of my personality as a teacher: my worry about whether I'm pleasing others. It's the unhealthy flip side of wanting to care for others effectively.

To combat this thinking, it's important for me to know that people who want to give to others effectively work to care for themselves effectively first; they also work to understand when to give and when to turn their focus inward. I've had to learn how to take a break and shut it all down, knowing that taking care of myself is also an important responsibility.

Each time I decide to rest and take the time I need, I have to remember I am doing what is best for myself and that this is important. Very important. Even if it feels uncomfortable, it is good to know that this discomfort is a part of the process of subverting the unhealthier side of my desire to fix, control, and please.

Reflection: *Taking a break when needed shouldn't have to be a decision we weigh for very long; however, when we find ourselves trying to push against our bodies' demand for rest, it is good to question why we are resisting this need. May we recognize whatever truth lies behind our resistance to taking care of ourselves and do what we can to make progress in the direction of self-care.*

On Outward Burnout

"M." was my department chair in my first year of teaching and someone I admired for her intelligence, confidence, and calm. I also looked up to her because she was an actual real adult, where I was a kid living in a messy apartment with three roommates. One night, while staying at school late to plan lessons, M. stopped in my classroom doorway. When I looked up, she placed her hand against the doorframe and lingered for a moment. Her calm presence was there with her. "Go home," she said. "You're going to burn yourself out."

At that moment, I felt chastened and hurt. I had heard of this supposed "teacher burnout" as a graduate student, but the young and know-it-all (read: afraid) teacher that I was, thought, "Ha! These typical jaded older teachers. She doesn't understand what *I* have to do for *my* students. And she doesn't know *me*. What I'm *capable* of."

But M. did know me. She might have even known I would respond this way. And I think she also knew a definition of burnout that I couldn't have understood at the time. Whenever I heard of burnout in graduate school and the culture at large, I imagined a wilted, exhausted thing who could no longer lift their head from their desk. This is certainly something I've experienced, but what M.

might have meant that night was what I came to know later: that "all we do" as teachers can significantly damage our ability to be present in other areas of our lives, thereby preventing us from valuable, meaningful experiences and opportunities outside of the classroom. A burned-out teacher might still be able to teach, but not without burning up time for everything else.

Although I was smarting from M.'s comment, I knew she was speaking the truth, even if I didn't want to hear it. I watched the way she operated in her classroom and throughout her day, and I compared this to how I operated. I was full of nerves, experiencing emotional highs and lows, and eating cold soup with a spoon from a can I stored in my desk drawer. M. was calm, steady, and present for her students, who accorded her great respect and admiration. I listened to her talk about her full life outside of school.

You'd think this reflection ends with me understanding a kind of outward burnout and telling you how I put a stop to it. Sadly, however, I was only finally willing to make changes to the way I managed my teaching life when I got to the point where I'd lost out on enough opportunities and experiences and felt sufficiently cornered enough to make a change. I am sometimes almost haunted, and surely bewildered, by the times I gave a firm "no" to family and friends because of "my teaching."

The good news is that as I've slowly made changes over the years to experience my life outside of the classroom, the more these opportunities have flourished (marriage, children, family, friendships, writing, art, and music, in my case) and *demanded* that I reconsider how I teach. I now have people and things in my life I value as much as I value my teaching, thus creating a kind of naturally imposed work/life balance.

I'm glad I began focusing more on my life outside of the classroom. And how satisfying it is to know that all I've added to my life on the "outside," I've been able to bring back "in." I can now connect with my students about my new life experiences *as well as* through my planning and implementation of the content I teach. I also feel better rested and less stressed. In fact, it is absolutely true, though counterintuitive, that the more time, energy, love, and effort I've poured into other areas of my life the more the attributes of teachers like M.—effectiveness, composure, and confidence—become my own. I become more like those I admire.

Reflection: *My role as a teacher is one of many roles I play and does not need to be so central that it saps the growth and health of my life outside the classroom. Today I will begin to look for new opportunities to use my time and energy outside of the classroom and observe the positive effects that will surely come.*

On the Special Effect of
Our Friendships with Colleagues

Our relationships with other teachers and how
we treat each other matters to us because they give us
comfort, respite, and a way to de-stress.

But what's more, as an unexpected effect, I've noticed
these relationships matter to our students too.

I always note my students' smiles and the glow
in their eyes whenever I mention my friendships
with teachers they know. Curiously, they've always
reacted this way, and over the years, I think I've
learned why.

First, students want to understand their teachers as
social creatures and as human beings who can operate
outside of lesson-teaching. This helps them build trust in
us and humanizes the force behind whatever it is we are
telling them is important to learn.

Secondly, and perhaps even more importantly, I
think students' understanding that we have meaningful
relationships in the school community reminds them
they are somewhere safe and good.

By making our adult relationships visible, we are
letting our students know that their school is a place
where adults care for each other and a place where adults

are thriving, much like the way we hope our students will thrive.

It can be especially powerful for students, too, when a fellow teacher and I can share in a student's success, for then the student is receiving double praise from two adults who have collaborated in support of their well-being.

It is surely a powerful thing for students to know that the adults in their lives are working together to demonstrate their care for them, their peers, and each other.

Reflection: *We not only have the opportunity to support our fellow teachers. We can also demonstrate our commitment to our school community through the relationships we build. May I look for opportunities to demonstrate the way I care for my school community as a gift to myself and to the students who look up to me.*

On Slowing Down and Seeing Clearly

My teacher friends and I have joked that, after a while, students start to blur together. Sometimes I get a kick out of students who happily remind me of students past. But on the other hand, this phenomenon can also make me feel jaded when I've been in the profession long enough to feel like I'm teaching copies of the same students over and over.

As a parent, I'd be horrified to hear that my children's teachers have ever seen them this way, but I think this phenomenon points to the fact that sometimes we can get overwhelmed with teaching to such a degree that we lose out on the rich experience of seeing each whole person in front of us. We start to see our students in a kind of teacher shorthand, as in, "Yeah, I've had this type of student before."

Recently, I was giving directions to my class, and I realized I wasn't even looking my students in the eye. I was talking to a class, just another class, an amorphous group, and I noticed I was speaking to the air somewhere out in front of me. I suddenly felt very detached. I didn't like it. It didn't feel right, and though I'd likely experienced this detachment before, this was the first time I really caught myself in the midst of it.

After some reflection about how the year was going and sensing I wasn't really bringing the kind of energy I'd planned, I concluded that this feeling was telling me I needed to focus more on my students and to do so individually. Armed with the belief that connecting one-on-one with students is one of the most powerful tools we have as teachers, I tried to think of a quick way to get reconnected.

Meeting with a student later that day, I paused and took a slow breath, and I physically and mentally tried to bring myself into the present. I focused on listening. And then, weirdly, by trying to center myself in the present, I instantly felt more attentive to meeting that students' needs. It was good to be talking to a person again and not just doing my thing to get through a lesson. I also felt a wave of relief; this was yet another reminder that connecting with students is what's really meaningful. It's the best part of the job.

Reflection: *When it comes down to it, my presence and connection to my students are what matter on any given school day. Even if they're the only things I can count as having gone right that day, I can call that a successful day of school. Taking a moment to become more present for this very task is a quick way to get back to the simple act that perhaps defines our teaching: being there.*

On "Wellness" that Asks Too Much of Us

Recently, I signed up for an email-based wellness program out of curiosity. The idea behind the program was that certain daily actions would benefit the subscriber's life, mostly by doing kind acts for others.

While I certainly don't disagree with the idea that giving to those around us can bring purpose and joy to our lives, it occurred to me that, as a teacher, I could stand to focus a little less on others and put more focus on restoring myself.

A day in my teaching life can include multiple hours of planning lessons I think my students will enjoy and find useful while also making modifications to that lesson to meet as many of their individual needs as I can. Then, of course, there's the teaching itself. Later that day, I could be eating a twenty-minute lunch while grading, then helping a student walk through a challenging time while assisting in coordinating a support system over the phone or by email. I am likely also responding to emails to help clarify assignments and take care of other logistics, mostly in support of my students. I think of this as a pretty normal school day, and you probably do too.

Too often, I feel compelled to work overtime on behalf of my students and school, even to the point of making sacrifices elsewhere in my life. Therefore, the last thing

I should want for my well-being is to, say, write letters to five friends to tell them how much I appreciate them or join a new cause or start an online fundraising campaign or look for someone in need, and reach out to them.

And yet, I've done these very things. I've turned to these actions, quite valuable and useful in themselves, and added them to my already bursting to-do list hoping they'd bring some sort of relief. Too often, however, the needed relief didn't arrive or was short-lived.

My daily routine is already loaded with ways to support others. My work is fundamentally based in public service— above and beyond, in fact. Once I discover that the benefits of giving are always available to me in my professional life, and I approach my work as such, I can turn to the kind of self-care that benefits me personally and provides real relief: that which feels restorative, relaxing, resting, healing, and, maybe most importantly, gives me a break from actions that mirror the authentic, meaningful giving of my teaching life.

Reflection: *Today I will consider this question: how can I approach my teaching as if it were my fundamental act of giving and care so that my time spent away from the classroom could be a time for restoration, rest, and focus on what, outside of my teaching, makes my life whole and full?*

On a Deeper Self-Care

When I am feeling overwhelmed, anxious, uncomfortable, or stressed about my teaching life, I find it helpful, first, to note the kind of stress I'm experiencing. Is it a problem that requires a simple reset? Or are there more significant issues at play that involve distressing emotions?

When I've had a tough day with students, or I'm reeling from hours of planning or grading, I'm usually in need of a reset. This consists of self-care methods that are available to us everywhere.

However, I find that many of these suggestions could be applied to nearly any profession. Teaching, it seems, can sometimes require a deeper level of self-care, which I see as an ongoing practice to sustain, protect, or enrich myself in the midst of the challenges of our field.

Emotions such as fear and anger come up in our teaching lives, and for good reason: educating students can be difficult and emotional work. We are regularly confronted with heartbreaking stories from our students, stark inequities, educational mandates we may disagree with, as well as pressures and expectations for student achievement.

Further, situations that may normally require a simple reset can go unchecked when I can't seem to take a breath, and what was once a minor stressor ends up producing feelings the reset won't quite fix.

I need to be able to face these challenges effectively too, just as much as I need to be rested and restored with traditional self-care.

Here are some deeper self-care practices I find sustaining and enriching, and that provide the kind of stability and relief I need as I face the work we do.

Deeper self-care, for me, is asking for help or speaking up when my gut says I should.

Deeper self-care is identifying my feelings honestly, communicating them to trusted colleagues, and considering how to approach a problem with a healthy consideration of all involved.

Deeper self-care is recognizing how I am internalizing the expectations of others, then taking small steps to break these patterns without being hard on myself.

Deeper self-care is not being hard on myself.

I am even practicing deeper self-care when I stand up for the needs of others, especially the vulnerable. One of the stresses of teaching for me is seeing something I know is wrong and feeling powerless to change it.

We need a lot of support as teachers, both on the surface and deep within. I've found that caring for myself as an educator can go as "deep" as I want it to, and the more willing I am to reset when needed as well as practice a deeper care, the more confident, balanced, and fulfilled I feel in this profession I love.

Reflection: *There are many ways to care for myself as a teacher. I can always find a temporary solution when I need to get through a hard day. I can also care for myself as a teacher through healthy practices of communication and self-reflection. Today I will try to identify my specific self-care needs and take actions to help me meet them.*

On Our Influence

When I am teaching my students something new,
I often wonder when I learned that same skill or lesson
myself, but I find this difficult to pin down.

I try to summon memories of former teachers and
what they've taught me, but this soon becomes a blur of
various moments, feelings, events, and faces over many
years, all significant in their own way.

One of the miraculous things about knowledge is that
once we gain it, it folds itself so imperceptibly into our
consciousness that we feel it has always been there,
a natural fact.

Once knowledge is *ours*, it is hard to recall the many
steps and stages, setbacks, and progress that define the
process of learning.

As teachers, this means we must face the reality
that our names and faces may eventually fade from
many of our students' memories, or we get mixed up
with that other teacher from another year, or our
classrooms are only remembered for something we
don't recall ourselves.

And perhaps this is where the art of teaching lies: to
create conditions that allow our students to do the thing
that seemed so difficult before and to do it with a sense of

ownership and pride that lets me know they don't quite remember a time when they couldn't.

To find satisfaction in this is where the wisdom of teaching lies: to allow our students this privilege of possessing knowledge without the need for recognition, just as we know what we've done for them—our planning, patience, strategy, and support—will be a part of their lives forever.

We are like proud parents who keep their unnoticed hands on their children's backs as they ride their first bicycles, beaming with confidence, self-possession, and joy.

Reflection: *It is humbling to think that although we are front and center for our students now, in the long run, our lessons, engagement, and support will be almost imperceptible for many of our students as they make their way in the world. May I consider this truth as a way to temper my drive for recognition, to lessen some form of intensity, or to experiment with how a behind-the-scenes role can empower those I teach.*

On Where We Stand

It wasn't until I became a father that I realized how much teachers really mean to me.

My son's and daughter's teachers have about as much face time with my children during the week as I do, if not more, and I now understand how dependent parents and caretakers are on their children's teachers, how much we trust them to care for and foster their growth.

From the perspective of a teacher, however, I rarely step back to recognize this, but it is good for me to remember that my job stands directly alongside one of the most powerful and meaningful human relationships, that of parent and child.

We teachers exist in the psyches of all parents, even if it's in the background of their daily lives. We play a leading role in the hopes, dreams, and fears they have for their children.

Perhaps only pediatricians or nurses can make a similar claim.

I like to remember how remarkable and special the responsibility of a teacher is. That we've chosen this profession says something important about us—that we value and are willing to work for the vulnerable, both the student in our care as well as the parent who has entrusted us with their child.

Reflection: *Through our teaching, we hold a meaningful place in the lives, hearts, and minds of students, parents, and caretakers. May I remember where I stand in relation to these powerful family dynamics.*

On the Simple Constancy of Teachers

One of the great gifts we give our students is our consistency. Our regular routines and schedules, even those dictated by the school bell, can offer order, structure, and constancy that some students may not get elsewhere and most students require.

Because of our unique role as someone who shows up and is there to help—a simple definition of "all we do"—it is possible we are one of the most regular forms of attention and care our students experience, however brief our contact might be.

This consistency is especially significant for students who are in crisis.

Students who have experienced trauma are susceptible to stress and anxiety when they encounter situations that mirror the confusion or chaos of whatever harm they've experienced. Our classrooms, therefore, can be a space for calm, healing, and safety.

Students who have experienced rejection, whatever that may be, have a chance, through their teachers, to experience an adult in their lives who will not ignore or leave them when they are struggling or purely just being themselves.

These day-in, day-out efforts open us up to the many kinds of relationships we can build with our students, but I think our constancy comes first. I always notice how much students warm up to me after the first month or so, though I often think it should be sooner. But then I realize it's likely they're waiting to see what they're going to get from me, not once, not occasionally, but consistently.

Reflection: *Our students reap the benefits of our being there at the first bell and the last. By the very nature of our jobs, we teachers offer a routine of care and assistance, and this is free to them and regular, and what we do best. Today I will look for ways to continue establishing the simple act of constancy in my classroom, for it can be enough to impact my students deeply.*

On Recognition

I've had to struggle with and reflect on my desire for more recognition as a teacher. Unlike those who work in the private sector, tangible rewards are difficult to come by for educators. Our jobs do not include more traditional incentives like bonuses and promotions.

I suppose I should have known this going into the profession, but as someone who likes to be recognized and rewarded, I've had to come to terms with the fact that external rewards for teachers are mostly unavailable (not that I agree) and that developing meaningful relationships, experiencing personal growth, and finding an internal sense of value are the available rewards for educators, and, from my perspective, can be more fulfilling and sustainable.

Admittedly, it's taken some time for me to understand this. For most of my career, I've been on the hunt to please or impress my administrators, other teachers, parents, and students. However, I've found that when I am pushing in this direction, I end up realizing my hunger for recognition is unfulfillable and that there is only the endless striving for that next scrap of attention.

And because there is no material incentive at the end of this chase—other than kind words, a thank-you note, a gift card, or being asked to join every imaginable committee—these efforts are nothing if not self-serving. What's more, the failure to find the perfect amount of recognition as a teacher ends up putting me in a "no one understands how much I do" sort of mood or worse, the "that teacher gets whatever they want, and they don't work as hard as I do" mood, and both are the opposite of feeling validated.

Therefore, I've had to consider it an act of self-care to learn how to find fulfillment in less tangible ways. I've had to learn how to accept the rewards and benefits of our profession as they are, even as I keep one eye trained on the ways I can contribute to economic justice for teachers.

Usually, the rewards available to me now are things I know are satisfying for me, but they're parts of the job I take for granted. I have to remember how deeply moving my relationships with students can be and how much these relationships have informed who I am and how I see the world. I have to remember the great pleasure of helping my students find joy in learning new things. I have to remember how many of my students are now out in the world likely using skills I've taught them for their benefit. I have to remember there is a strong sense of accomplishment in seeing myself become a more effective teacher and person as I grow in my care, compassion, and skill. I have to remember that not every professional gets to experience these things as frequently as I can.

These are the kinds of recognition that have no arrival place: to develop new and significant relationships, to find joy in seeing students fall in love with learning, and to let myself grow in heart, mind, in spirit are the work of an entire lifetime, and there's enough for each of us to have in abundance.

Reflection: *Our professional lives provide opportunities to foster the well-being of others as well as our own. Though it may be difficult at times to go without the material rewards we desire (and deserve), the act of receiving the benefits we do reap can be sustaining, lasting, and life-changing.*

On Our Legacies

I feel fortunate to have learned from the example of the many teachers and champions for education in my family, including cousins, a dear aunt, and my father who served tirelessly and wisely for many, many years as president of the board of education in the town where I grew up.

I am thinking today, however, about my mother's legacy as a teacher. An absolute powerhouse of a special education teacher, she is one of the educators I admire most. Though I'd been in her classroom at other times, in the last few years before she retired, I had a chance to observe her through a teacher's eyes.

While I don't remember the entire lesson she taught that day, the moment that sticks out in my mind now is the laughter and joy of her students as they participated in class and engaged meaningfully and humorously with her.

My mom was able to make time for playfulness in her lessons while also managing to permanently alter the lives of her students for the better. Just as her students' joy is what sticks out to me from my visit, I wonder if this is also what her students remember too.

When I think back on the teachers who meant the most to me, I use my heart. I quickly feel the presence of those who encouraged playfulness, the ones who recognized me, the ones who showed me I could trust them or made being in their class feel like the most interesting place to be. And I often think of these experiences before I consider the who, when, and where of all the influential academic lessons I've learned.

It seems to me, then, that we have a double legacy as teachers. We are transmitting our humanity to our students as much as our knowledge and expertise. That I immediately use my heart and feelings when I consider my favorite teachers are telling about how deep this work goes.

As a teacher, it is freeing to know that there are so many ways to leave a lasting imprint on our students. This helps me lighten up in my teaching and focus on virtues beyond my often intense focus on lessons. My mom, an expert in her field, knew this. Her laughing, joyful students are a good example for me when I am tightly bound to the regimen of curriculum.

Keeping my mother's example in mind, it also occurs to me that our legacies are not only for our students, but for the teachers who work beside us as well as those who will come after us; for, after all, we are each other's greatest encouragement and support, the single most important group of people we can go to when we are in need of help, and part of a long lineage of wisdom about how to care for others—those of us who have been strong enough to choose this incredible, complex work we do.

Reflection: *While we often don't know the specific effects we've had on our students, we can reflect on our own experiences as students to recall the lasting impacts teachers make. Today I will reflect on my own relationships with former teachers as a way of refocusing my teaching and presence toward what I ultimately want my students to take away from their time spent in my care.*

About the Author

Peter Mishler is an award-winning educator and poet.
A high school English teacher for thirteen years, he has
twice been named Teacher of the Year at schools in
New York and Kansas. His first collection of poems,
Fludde, published by Sarabande Books in 2018, won the
prestigious Kathryn A. Morton Prize in Poetry. Also a
regular contributor to *Literary Hub*, he lives in Kansas
with his wife and two children.

Author photo by Justin Boening

Acknowledgments

Thank you to the many students, teachers, and administrators for the friendships, experiences, and professional opportunities that have informed this writing. You've made my life and worldview more whole.

Thank you to my wife, Bridget, and my mother-in-law, Jean, for your encouragement and support with the writing. To my father-in-law, Dennis, for showing me the Circle.

Thank you to my children for belonging to yourselves so beautifully and to my children's teachers for artfully demonstrating the profound value of education.

Thank you to Aaron Schwartz for a helpful observation.

To my teachers and teaching mentors, I have thought about you all with warmth and joy during the writing of this book.

Thank you to Patty Rice, Lucas Wetzel, and the rest of the AMP team responsible for bringing this book to life: Julie Barnes, Jasmine Lim, and Carol Coe. Thank you for your vision and guidance. It is a high honor to work with you.